From Gatekeeper to Advocate: Transforming the Role of the School Counselor

From Gatekeeper to Advocate: Transforming the Role of the School Counselor

PHYLLIS J. HART
MARYANN JACOBI

College Entrance Examination Board
New York, 1992

The College Board is a nonprofit membership organization committed to maintaining academic standards and broadening access to higher education. Its more than 2,700 members include colleges and universities, secondary schools, university and school systems, and education associations and agencies. Representatives of the members elect the Board of Trustees and serve on committees and councils that advise the College Board on the guidance and placement, testing and assessment and financial aid services it provides to students and educational institutions.

In all of its book publishing activities the College Board endeavors to present the works of authors who are well qualified to write with authority on the subject at hand and to present accurate and timely information. However, the opinions, interpretations, and conclusions of the authors are their own and do not necessarily represent those of the College Board; nothing contained herein should be assumed to represent an official position of the College Board or any of its members.

The Achievement Council is a nonprofit organization aimed at increasing academic achievement among minority and low-income students in California. Since 1984, the council has worked with schools toward school improvement and increased student achievement, and has shared what it learns with policymakers, encouraging them to move in more promising directions.

Copies of this book may be ordered from College Board Publications, Box 886, New York, New York 10101-0886. The price is $10.95.

Editorial inquiries concerning this book should be directed to Editorial Office, College Board, 45 Columbus Avenue, New York, New York 10023-6992.

Library of Congress Catalog Number: 92-074668

ISBN: 0-87447-478-7

Printed in the United States of America

9 8 7 6 5 4 3 2 1

To the many, many students whose untapped genius inspired me to shift from gatekeeper to advocate.

Contents

Foreword

Phyllis Hart has been a key adviser to the College Board on matters related to the educational guidance of students since she served as vice chair of the Board's Commission on Precollege Guidance and Counseling. The 1986 report of that commission, *Keeping the Options Open*, which reflects Phyllis's leadership and the beliefs we share with her about the educational needs of all students, has often been referred to as "the bible" for the reform and improvement of educational guidance.

Since that time, Phyllis has remained an active participant in the College Board. Currently, she chairs the National Guidance Committee for our EQUITY 2000 initiative; coordinates our Lilly Endowment-funded project, "Keeping the Options Open: Continued"; and provides us with critical advice and guidance as we define an appropriate role for the College Board on behalf of middle schools and their students.

When I read Phyllis's 1991 report to the DeWitt Wallace-Reader's Digest Fund, "From Gatekeeper to Advocate: Transforming the Role of the School Counselor," a report that renews and reminds us of the vision in *Keeping the Options Open*, I quickly asked whether the College Board could take responsibility for publishing an appropriate adaptation of the report and then disseminating it widely to College Board member counselors and others concerned with the educational guidance of our students. We are very grateful that permission was granted by the DeWitt Wallace-Reader's Digest Fund and that we can now share this timely and important contribution.

Thank you, Phyllis for your continuing support for the work of the College Board and, more importantly, for your advocacy on behalf of all students. And thank you DeWitt Wallace-Reader's Digest Fund for supporting this important work.

DONALD M. STEWART
President
The College Board

Acknowledgments

The authors gratefully acknowledge the DeWitt Wallace-Reader's Digest Fund for underwriting this study. To help American youth achieve their educational and career potential, the Fund invests nationwide in programs to: improve schools, strengthen organizations and programs that serve youth, encourage ties between schools and communities and promote educational and career-related reform at the national level.

The authors also extend a special thanks to Mildred Hudson, program director at the DeWitt Wallace-Reader's Digest Fund, whose commitment to strong counseling programs for all students inspired us. Also, deep appreciation to Kati Haycock, director of the Education Roundtable, American Association of Higher Education (founder and first executive director of The Achievement Council) for assisting us in shaping this work.

Introduction

Recently published data make it very clear that U.S. young people possess neither the knowledge nor the skills that they need to participate intelligently in either the civic or economic life of this country. By age 17, only half of our young people can solve simple math problems using decimals, fractions, or percents; fewer than half can summarize a paragraph from a simple text such as an encyclopedia; and fewer than one-quarter can write even a slightly persuasive letter. The average high school graduate can recite basic facts, but never learned to analyze or draw conclusions from them.

But if our current system works poorly for the average U.S. student, it is failing miserably for poor and minority students who, by age 17, are equipped on average with skills about the same as those of the average white 13-year-old. Contrary to popular myth, however, this gap is not simply the result of poverty, poor health, and family problems. Rather, by creating a system of structured inequalities, U.S. educators routinely turn small gaps into larger ones. Our education system gives the least to those who need the most—then turns around and blames lower performance on the students and their families.

With strong leadership from business and government, much energy is currently being devoted to efforts to restructure the educational system in ways that will improve educational outcomes. There is now widespread agreement on practices seldom mentioned even a few years ago, such as rigorous national standards, national performance-based examinations, and rewards for improved performance. But there is a glaring, gaping hole in current reform planning: counseling, guidance, and course placement practices. If this gap is not filled, our guidance and placement systems will continue to do what they do now: under-

1

estimate student potential and depress academic achievement, especially among minority and poor students. And the goal of all the reform
planning will be thwarted.

This report proposes a strategy for filling in the hole, based on a
clear vision of what counseling and guidance could be, and with a clear
understanding of the current situation. The vision proposed here is of
schools where every student is challenged and supported to achieve at
the highest possible level, and where counselors:

- Believe in the capacity of all students to learn at high levels;
- Assume a leadership role in keeping the school and the community
  focused on promoting and enabling student achievement;
- Create and coordinate networks of service providers; and
- are held accountable—along with others in the school—for results.

If counselors are to adhere to this new framework, their training
must be improved. Accordingly, this report provides an overview of
current counselor preparation and proposes much-needed changes.
However, although these changes would be helpful, they would by no
means be sufficient to bring about necessary changes in school or professional practice. Hence, this report calls for an effort that would focus
on whole schools and place guidance within an analytic framework
based on a consideration of student needs. Counseling and guidance
programs and activities would be designed to promote student achievement; they would include not only designated counselors, but anyone
in the school or community who could contribute to meeting student
needs.

The report suggests both long- and short-term approaches and re-
views some of the efforts currently underway in each category. Short-
term activities are aimed at filling a void in a school's array of support
services by providing immediate assistance to currently enrolled students. Long-term approaches strive for systemic change; they seek to
improve student achievement by modifying the underlying organizational structure and philosophy of individual schools and the broader
education system.

Can we change counseling and placement systems? Yes we can. It
won't be easy, because these practices are long entrenched, and the
profession is highly resistant to change. But there is a strong wind
blowing across the education system: a wind that is sweeping in some
new thinking about what is possible, and blowing away some of the
cobwebs that have clouded the thinking of practicing educators for
decades. We worry, however, that those winds won't blow down the
high walls that have been built around the counseling and guidance
function. That is the danger. But that, too, is the opportunity.

Setting the Context: A Troubled Education System

The publication of *A Nation at Risk* in 1983 dramatically raised the country's consciousness about the deficiencies of the public school system. Since that time, a steady stream of reports has revealed that large numbers of U.S. students lack the skills and knowledge they need to become productive members of our society. By age 17, only half of our young people can solve simple math problems using decimals, fractions, or percents; fewer than half can summarize a paragraph from a simple text such as an encyclopedia; and fewer than one-quarter can write even a slightly persuasive letter. The average high school graduate can recite everyday facts, but never learned to think about or analyze them. When compared to students elsewhere, U.S. students lag far behind their Asian and European counterparts.

Results are even worse for minority students and those from low-income families. Although these students typically enter school only slightly behind other students, they fall further and further behind as they progress through the grades. By age 17, the average black or Hispanic student's skills are about the same as those of the average white 13-year-old.

The fiscal and human costs of such discrepancies are severe. Work force projections suggest that close to half of all jobs in the twenty-first century will require college degrees, yet only a small proportion of black or Hispanic students will have earned baccalaureates. Because about one-third of the work force will be nonwhite by that time, the gap between the requirements of the job market and the educational level of the work force will be considerable. A 1989 report by the National Association of Student Financial Aid Administrators (NASFAA) and the American Council on Education (ACE) offered the following prediction of what will happen without significant changes:

> a significant percentage of the class of 2001 will be alienated from school by sixth grade, on the street by age 16. Many will not only join an underclass of citizens living in poverty, they will become . . . individuals who do not work, pay taxes, vote, or concern themselves with others, but instead drain resources. . . . Henry Levin of Stanford University estimated several years ago that the cost of school dropouts, current ages 25–34, amounted conservatively to $77 billion every year. (p. 1)

Indeed, our very future as a nation—economic and otherwise—is clearly at stake.

The Causes of Underachievement: Myths versus Reality

Most people assume that the gap separating poor and minority students from other young Americans is attributable primarily to the students or their families. They point to poverty, poor health, and family disintegration as the root causes of underachievement. However, although these problems do make learning more difficult (and should be addressed), they do not make high levels of achievement impossible. But rather than giving these youngsters the challenges and support they need to excel, the education system gives the least to those who need the most. Through a system of structured inequalities, educators routinely turn small gaps into larger ones, then turn around and blame the results on the children and their families.

The process begins in the earliest years of schooling, when children first receive messages about their worth and value. Typically, children in kindergarten or first grade are labeled according to their facility with language and are then placed in different groups— bluebirds, redbirds, and buzzards. It is at this moment that students begin getting different kinds of education and different messages about their worth. The "top" groups are exposed to interesting books, which they discuss with one another in their group sessions. The lower groups spend their time completing boring drills and repetitive exercises. While children in the top group are beginning to learn thinking skills, children in the bottom group are circling "m's" and "p's" on ditto after ditto.

According to Haycock and Navarro (1988), "By the time they reach second or third grade, youngsters assigned to these low groups have learned some enduring lessons: school is boring, and teachers don't think kids like me can do much" (p. 19). These practices continue despite clear evidence that schools often confuse acquired skills with innate ability and despite clear evidence that grouping and tracking harm a majority of students and don't truly help anybody (Oakes, 1985).

The groups that are formed in elementary school harden into tracks in junior and senior high school: honors, advanced, college preparatory, regular, average, and remedial. By sorting students on the basis of perceived ability, tracking becomes a self-reinforcing, and even a self-amplifying, system. Students who are perceived as having high ability (but in reality simply acquire good skills) are exposed to the most talented teachers, the most rigorous curriculum, and the highest level of stimulation and challenge. Students perceived to have low ability are exposed to less talented teachers, a curriculum somewhere between easy and empty, and low levels of stimulation. Parental expectations are tracked, as well, and parents of students labeled "low ability" start believing that their children are not as bright as others, thereby contributing to the cycle.

Haycock and Navarro (1988) stated:

> Into the education of poor children, we put less of everything we believe makes a difference. Less-experienced and well-trained teachers. Less instructional time. Less-rich and well-balanced curricula. Less well-equipped facilities. And less of what may be most important of all: a belief that these youngsters can really learn. (pp. 3-4)

The consequences of being assigned to an average or remedial track are severe and long-lasting. Rosenbaum (1976) summarized the effects of tracking in this way:

> The college tracks create a culture of accomplishment, where teachers must expect to discern differences among students, and where students must expect that their accomplishments will help them survive future selections. In contrast, the noncollege tracks create a culture of fatalism, where teachers expect to discern no differences in students' accomplishments, and where students expect that no amount of effort or accomplishment pays off. College-track students learn that social institutions are responsive to their efforts, but noncollege-track students learn that these institutions do not respond. (p. 185)

Oakes (1985) found that high school graduates who were educated in the remedial track had just as low employment rates as high school dropouts. Further, students in the lower tracks dropped out at higher rates. Even after controlling for race and income, students in other than college-preparatory classes have a 20 percent greater chance of dropping out of school.

Disproportionate numbers of minority and low-income students are placed in the lower groups and tracks. Oakes (1985) reported that minority students are twice as likely as white students to be assigned to slow or remedial classes, even after taking into account the variance due to standardized test scores and other "objective" measures. Although teachers claim that tracking is based on objective standards, both Oakes (1985) and Rosenbaum (1976) found that subjective appraisals by school personnel strongly influence track assignments. Tracking is probably the single largest cause of the achievement gap. Minority and poor students simply are not taught many of the things that our society considers important, and that are included in national tests.

To make matters worse, however, large numbers of students have basic misconceptions or gaps in their understanding of the education system and its implications for their life planning. For example, junior high school students whose parents or other family members have not attended college often feel that college is not an option for them. When they are asked what careers they have chosen, many of these students (including low-income and minority students) respond by mentioning careers that require a college degree, but they do not plan to attend college. They believe that college is only for the wealthy, or only for those who get straight A's on their report cards, or only for those who receive a high score on a mysterious test. Many students do not understand the relationship between educational and life planning. They especially do not understand how the choices they make as junior high or high school students will affect their educational and career options in the future.

As a result of these gaps and misconceptions, few students (especially few low-income or minority students) will vigorously object to being assigned to a vocational or general track. Neither will they demand to be placed in a college-preparatory track. Because college is rarely discussed in other tracks, the students' beliefs are never addressed or corrected, and they remain unaware of their options.

Further, few students and parents realize the devastating social consequences of being assigned to one of the lower tracks. Rosenbaum (1976) found that students were not making informed choices when they agreed to enter a noncollege track. These students and their parents accepted the school's assurances that they were in the "right" group for them and that they would have ample career and educational opportunities in the future. They did not know that being assigned to a general or vocational track greatly diminished their chances of attending college. He wrote:

> Believing that noncollege tracks offer good opportunities, students accept and internalize the role and status that accompany their track position. Only much later do they realize that they were deceived and that they should not have conformed so fully and accepted the negative evaluations so readily. But by then it is too late, for they have already adapted themselves to the restricted role and low status of the noncollege tracks, and this role and status are part of their self-concept. (p. 183)

The Counselor's Pivotal Role

School guidance and counseling practices contribute to the perpetuation of educational inequality by supporting tracking systems and by failing to correct students' misconceptions about the meaning of such assignments. Rosenbaum (1976) characterized guidance in middle and high schools as "vague misdirection," particularly with regard to track assignments. Written descriptions of various tracks (e.g., precollege or general) do not clearly differentiate the tracks or describe the outcomes associated with them. Students' direct access to counselors is typically limited, and Rosenbaum suggested that counselors' dual roles of "informing and advising" lead them to:

> provide a student with the kind of information that they judge to be most appropriate to the student's ability. . . . In actual practice, information and advice become related so that students are provided with the kind of information that will ensure that the counselor's advice is chosen. (pp. 117–120)

As a result, students' choices are not necessarily based on full information about the long-term imlications of their decisions.

Tracking systems encourage counselors to disseminate information selectively. For example, they may make sure that students they consider to be "college material" are enrolled in a college-preparatory curriculum and are knowledgeable about financial aid and admission procedures. Other students, however, do not receive this advice and information. Even if these other students want to attend college, they may not have access to the information about admission requirements, testing, and financial aid, which is crucial to achieving their aspirations.

Counselors may limit student achievement by denying students the opportunity to change into or remain in a precollege track. Rosenbaum (1976) described how this occurs:

The guidance counselors seem to have worked out strategies for persuading students to switch to, or remain in, a noncollege track. The main strategies in both cases are to disparage the student, stressing his lack of ability or his lack of motivation, and then to emphasize that the student's own behavior has made the counselor's decision inevitable. . . . The guidance counselor's second step is to conclude that the student's poor performance indicates that he belongs in a noncollege track. This inference is not inevitable . . . [but] this solution follows so directly from the track structure that none of the students ever think to question it. . . . Parents rarely become involved in track changes. . . . But even when parents support a student's efforts, they are not very effective, largely because of the educational difference between parents and counselors. (pp. 122–123)

Observing such practices, Hart and Mayes (1984) noted that counselors often become the "enforcers" of a school's philosophy by ensuring congruence between students' course choices and activities on the one hand and the offerings and expectations of the school on the other hand. For example, counselors in affluent school districts that send large numbers of students to college enroll most students in a precollege curriculum and discourage them from pursuing other paths. In contrast, counselors in inner-city school districts enroll few students in a precollege curriculum and most students in vocational or remedial courses. If the counselors encouraged more students to enroll in the precollege curriculum, the discrepancy between course availability and student demand would force the school to examine and modify its curricula. By not taking this step, counselors are enforcing the philosophy and expectations of the school and maintaining the status quo.

Through their activities, counselors either support or challenge their school's philosophy, structure, curriculum, and treatment of its students. Although counselors are often seen as peripheral to the mainstream of education, they in fact occupy a crucial position. For this reason, efforts to improve the nation's schools and create a more equitable system require careful consideration of guidance and counseling.

School Reform

The current school reform movement is actually a highly disparate collection of efforts intended to ameliorate the problems besetting the education system. Such efforts focus on a range of issues (e.g., curricular content, pedagogy, student behavior and well-being, public policy, and administrative and management practices), using a wide variety of models and approaches.

School-Based Management

Among the most popular of the reform strategies are efforts aimed at transferring authority and decision making from centralized district or statewide offices to local schools and communities. The school-based management approach reflects the belief that each school and community is unique, and that school personnel and community members should be empowered to decide how best to improve education.

School-based management models have been used for several years in parts of Massachusetts and Florida and were more recently implemented in Los Angeles, California. Unfortunately, early results are not encouraging. Dade County, Florida, has shown no changes in student achievement since the initiation of school-based management. An analysis of Boston schools showed that school-based management was not producing changes in teaching and curriculum (Citywide Educational Coalition, as summarized in Olson 1991). School-based management has been in operation in Los Angeles for less than three years and has not yet been evaluated, but observation and anecdotal evidence suggest that a similar trend is emerging. Perhaps it's simply too early to tell.

Coalition of Essential Schools

Under the leadership of Theodore Sizer of Brown University, the coalition of essential schools is another widely disseminated model of school reform. The model identifies five educational imperatives:

1. Give teachers and students the opportunity to work and learn in their own, appropriate ways;
2. Insist that students clearly exhibit mastery of their schoolwork;
3. Provide the proper incentives for students and teachers;
4. Focus the students' work on the use of their minds; and
5. Keep the structure simple and flexible (Sizer and Houston 1985, p. 1).

Like school-based management, the coalition emphasizes the importance of education models that are developed at the school level and in which students and teachers feel a strong sense of ownership. As a result, the coalition asks members to subscribe to a set of general principles but does not impose a particular set of programs or interventions. Coalition staff provide consultation and support services to member schools on request.

Comer Schools

The efforts of James Comer originated as a collaborative project between the Yale Child Study Center and the New Haven school system. This approach focuses on child development and relationship issues, recognizing that many children are unable to learn in school due to emotional, psychological, or behavioral problems (Comer 1986).

The solution lies in more attention to the "affective domain" (the environment in which the children are learning) through reorganization to increase the ability of teachers and staff to promote students' psychological well-being. Improved achievement, according to the Comer model, will follow. The school staff addresses the needs of children through a school governance team which brings school staff together to share in management and decision making. The Comer schools also emphasize parental involvement and involvement of mental health professionals to address student problems. Interventions or approaches that respond to each child's needs are planned and integrated into the educational process.

This approach has been effective in improving academic achievement among low-income and minority elementary school students and shows some promising results with secondary school students. The Comer model is in use by at least 16 inner-city school districts nationwide, and the New Jersey education department plans to introduce the model in urban schools statewide (Schmidt 1991).

Accelerated Schools

The accelerated schools model, developed by Henry Levin at Stanford University, has now been implemented in over 40 elementary schools serving large numbers of low-income and minority students. Traditionally, disadvantaged children have been assigned to remedial tracks, where the pace of teaching is relatively slow. As a result, children learn less, the educational gaps between remedial and mainstream students grow, and the children in remedial courses fall further and further behind their peers. In contrast, accelerated schools provide disadvantaged children with a more intense program (i.e., an accelerated program), with the goal of bringing students into the academic mainstream by the end of elementary school.

Accelerated schools incorporate a systemic change approach. In developing an accelerated program, participating schools assess curriculum, instructional methods, and school organization, and modify them as needed. The change process is guided by three principles: unity of purpose (emphasizing participation of all members of the school community and development of a shared vision statement and goals); empowerment and responsibility (enlarging the decision-making abilities and accountability of school staff and other members of the education community); and building on strengths (using schools' and students' strengths to "build bridges" to other areas that may need improvement). Preliminary results support the effectiveness of accelerated schools in promoting high levels of achievement among disadvantaged or at-risk youth.

In some ways, the accelerated schools approach is not directly relevant to this analysis. It focuses exclusively on elementary schools and does not specifically highlight the role of the school counselor. From another perspective, however, the accelerated schools model is noteworthy for its underlying philosophy and values. The model affirms the ability of each student to achieve at high levels and establishes high expectations for student achievement. In addition, the model focuses on equity issues in education.

The Kentucky Approach

With support from national business leaders, many states are considering a set of reforms similar to those adopted a few years ago by the Kentucky legislature in response to a court order. In many ways, the Kentucky approach is a hybrid: it combines an emphasis on statewide standards and tests and a school-based management approach whereby educators in the individual schools receive cash bonuses for progress in getting more students to meet the new standards, and penalties if they do not. It also adds some dimensions from the Comer model: a focus on meeting the health and social services needs of students and their families.

It is still too early to pass judgment on most of these efforts. One thing, however, is clear. Most of them totally overlook guidance and counseling. Few of the many attempts to explain what is wrong with the system and few attempts to improve education in grades K through 12 include counseling. These oversights represent a substantial number of lost opportunities for improving education by helping the nation's children to learn.

Including Counseling in Reform Strategies

Despite the general inattention paid to counseling, two reports do provide an excellent point of departure for an in-depth discussion and review of counseling's role in school reform. The first is the work of the Commission on Precollege Guidance and Counseling. This group, which was convened by the College Board in 1984, reviewed available research and interviewed school counselors, administrators, community members, and students. Its two-volume report, *Keeping the Options Open* (Commission on Precollege Guidance and Counseling 1986a and b), describes students' needs in relation to the condition of counseling, addresses equity issues, and provides a valuable set of recommendations. Its analysis assigns counseling a key role in school reform:

> The first year of investigation has left the commission with the broad impression that there is a considerable waste of human talent as a result of the ways our schools are now operated, and that the counseling and guidance functions in the schools can contribute significantly to reducing that waste. . . . If the rights of all children to learn and become self-sufficient citizens are to be respected, and the needs of society for educated men and women are to be met, students from poor and minority families must become more successful than they are now in high school and college. The place of guidance and counseling in schools can be significant in producing that result. (1986a, pp. vi–vii)

With support from the Lilly Endowment, the College Board and the National Association of College Admissions Counselors (NACAC) are sponsoring a program called "Strengthening Educational Guidance and Counseling in Schools." The program was developed in response to *Keeping the Options Open* and is specifically intended to implement the commission's recommendations in 10 school districts.

The program uses a training model that brings together teams of seven individuals from each district. Each team includes district administrators, school principals, teachers (in English and mathematics), and counselors. The teams discussed how to change academic outcomes, particularly for minority and poor students. Issues such as tracking and grouping, instructional practices, and the role of the counselor were discussed. Participants were also exposed to "school turn-around" people—individuals who have made a difference and improved the quality of education in their schools. Each team developed a vision statement, goals and objectives, and an action plan for addressing access and equity and improving academic outcomes in its district. The teams also completed an analysis of their districts' performance and problems, based on quantitative data as well as their own observations.

During the implementation phase, project staff made site visits to each district. In addition, each district is required to submit written reports about its progress. The teams met again in May of 1992, to celebrate their success and acknowledge the challenges that remain.

Although progress is uneven, preliminary findings from this project are encouraging. In Emporia, Virginia, for example, the number of black students enrolling in algebra has increased tenfold. In South Bend,

Indiana, one school admitted into a prealgebra course some minority students who did not meet the usual enrollment requirements. Subsequent evaluation indicated that these students actually received slightly higher grades on average than those who met the requirements. In San Jose, California, and Minneapolis, Minnesota, students begin to receive information about college as early as the sixth grade.

Participating schools addressed precollege guidance and counseling in different ways. Some focus primarily on the counselors' role, while others focus on teachers. Some address improving delivery of precollege guidance as well as improving instruction.

This effort is noteworthy for several reasons. First, interest in participation was extremely high. Over 300 districts applied in response to the call for proposals, although only 10 could be chosen. This indicates the increasing readiness of school districts nationwide to invest in educational reform, especially with regard to precollege guidance and counseling.

Second, the program provides a demonstration of how short-term and long-term approaches to educational reform can be implemented simultaneously. Each district was able to develop and implement new counseling interventions that led to improved student achievement within a relatively short time. Simultaneously, each district considered how to modify the manner in which its schools are organized and structured so that student achievement is maximized.

Third, the program was cosponsored by the College Board. Given the Board's national prominence, commitment to maintaining rigorous academic standards, and membership that is generally perceived to include the elite institutions of the U.S. education system, its involvement in this project sent an important message to the nation about the importance of correcting educational inequities and lent credibility to attempts to strengthen and modify precollege counseling and guidance.

The second is a 1986 report by the National College Counseling Project, sponsored by NACAC, entitled *Frontiers of Possibility*. It focused on college counseling in secondary and middle schools, including the distribution of college counseling resources and factors associated with effective college counseling. This report made a strong argument for college counseling programs to strengthen community linkages with families, business and civic organizations, and colleges and universities.

These major reports on counseling demonstrate the profusion of challenges facing the field but are optimistic about the potential for school guidance and counseling to make a meaningful difference in the lives of children. The case studies in Chapter 2 show how some counselors can make that difference, but many don't.

2

Counselors in Practice

Some counselors are far more successful than others in helping students to make informed decisions and to achieve their greatest potential. As the following narratives, adapted from actual case studies, show, counselors' effectiveness is influenced by many factors, including their own background, experience, and training; their expectations for their students; and the extent to which they are willing to "make waves," instead of accepting the status quo.

Three Counselors

Ruth

When Ruth began her career as a high school counselor 20 years ago, the student body at Kennedy High was entirely white. Most of the families were solidly middle class and aspired to even more for their children. Pushed by their parents, students regularly signed up for college-preparatory classes and visited the counseling center as necessary to obtain college information. Ruth had taught English at Kennedy before obtaining her pupil personnel credential, which enabled her to take "a step up" in the system.

In the beginning, most of Ruth's days were spent dealing with minor scheduling snafus, making certain that college catalogs were up-to-date, and counseling students with minor personal problems. She had plenty of time to keep up with changes in college admission requirements by reading reports and staying in touch with her favorite recruiters from college campuses.

Seven or eight years ago, the demographics in the neighborhoods surrounding Kennedy began to change, and Hispanic families began to replace many of the Anglo-American families. At first, the change was so slight that hardly anyone noticed, including Ruth. But she ultimately noticed signs of change. Conversations in the teachers' lunchroom turned frequently to fond—and often overblown—memories of "the kids we used to have." English-as-a-second-language courses began to exceed Honors English sections on the master schedule. Counselors got more requests from teachers, parents, and students to move students into easier courses than into harder ones. The counseling center received fewer visitors looking for college information than visitors looking for help with pressing personal and family needs.

Ruth's typical day was spent in search of clothing for a student who had none or counseling a student with an alcoholic single parent. The college information library of which she was once so proud became out-of-date through inattention. She still tried to provide good information about college to students who asked for it, but few did, and she didn't have the time or the inclination to think about why. Her job was to meet student needs—and this is what they thought they needed.

Once, a visitor to the school remarked that the advanced classes seemed to be full of white students, while the lower track classes were all filled with Hispanics. Ruth was caught by surprise: it had never occurred to her to think about the pattern or to wonder whether it might be part of a national problem. After all, she was placing students where she thought they would get the most appropriate education. Wasn't that her job? And neither students nor their parents seemed to object.

Richard

When Richard was in ninth grade, his counselor at all-black Riverside High took a special interest in him. Thinking he saw a spark of potential in the 15-year-old, the counselor moved Richard out of his general track classes and into a college-preparatory sequence. Richard himself wasn't at all sure about this at the time, and when things got tough—especially in algebra—he wondered if he could make it. But his counselor was always there for him, repeating over and over again, "Of course you can make it, Richard. You're at least as smart as anyone else at Riverside High." Richard did make it. And, as he went through the local university, he had a single goal: to become a high school counselor and help other students in the same way his counselor had made such a big difference for him.

In 1986, as a newly certified counselor, Richard sought a job in an inner-city high school and was pleased when he landed one at Central High School right away. The school was half black and half Hispanic, and few, if any, of the students had parents who had gone to college. This was just the challenge he had hoped for.

His first four days at Central were spent in meetings with the director of guidance and other counselors at the school as they prepared for the opening of the academic year. He was informed that he had a student load of 650: all of the freshmen who were assigned to the vocational and general tracks. The college counselor had responsibility for the 80 seniors in the college-preparatory track and their counterparts in the other grades.

When Richard asked why so few students were assigned to college-preparatory classes, the counselors just snickered and said that most had fourth-grade-level skills—hardly the stuff of future college students. Not one to give in easily, he asked whether some of his students could be reassigned later on if he thought they showed potential. The director of guidance just rolled her eyes.

For the first six months, Richard cherished some hope that he could begin to change things at Central—first for just a few students and maybe later for the entire student body. But it seemed that virtually everything in the school conspired to beat that hope out of him.

First, from day one, Richard was deluged with students who needed help with major crises in their lives. Although he had grown up in a tough area, his own experience and training proved woefully inadequate in dealing with these problems. He referred many of the students with the most severe problems to outside agencies, but never was really sure that they even got to their appointments. He didn't have time to check.

Second, the students themselves seemed totally uninvolved. Many of his referrals were from other teachers frustrated because the students never completed homework assignments. But when Richard tried to point out how important a good education was to their futures, the students typically responded, "What futures?" He might make progress one day with one student, but his schedule was so packed on the following days that he couldn't hang in there with the student to keep the pressure on.

Parents, too, were a frequent problem. They often kept their children out of school for reasons such as babysitting for younger siblings, without understanding the price their children were paying in the classroom. Many allowed their children to work late at night at local fast-food joints for spending money, instead of ensuring that their children got ample sleep. And when Richard tried to talk to the parents about these consequences, they typically responded by saying, "What can I do? I'm just thankful that he's not selling crack on some street corner."

Richard was totally overwhelmed by the size of his student load. In his counselor-training program he had learned a lot about good counseling techniques, but he never had a chance to use them. Virtually all of his time was spent on clerical tasks, monitoring the lunchroom, or in 10-minute crisis sessions with students. He had no time to be proactive at all.

From time to time, Richard thought about leaving the profession. He realized that he was becoming part of the problem rather than the solution, but he could think of no alternative. So he just gave up hope and stopped thinking about the larger picture. By lowering his expectations for students, he protected himself from the pain of daily disappointments.

Lynn

Lynn worked as an English teacher at Millay High for six years. In her sixth year, the principal asked her to become the school's college counselor. "It won't take you much time," he said. "Only about 5 percent of our students are college material."

Lynn's first year was a real eye-opener. To a certain extent, the principal was right: only a few students saw themselves as college material, so the demands on her time were small. But Lynn knew from her experience in teaching English that many within Millay's predominantly Hispanic and black student body had the potential to do college-level work: where were they?

Further, she began to wonder about what the school was doing for those who were in the college-preparatory track. During her first six months, she had a number of visits from Millay's "best and brightest," students who had compiled 3.9 grade-point averages and had gone on to UCLA. Every one of them was angry, though, at the woefully inadequate preparation they had received at Millay. When they compared what they knew—about English literature or science, for example—to the knowledge base of their fellow freshmen from the suburbs, they realized that they had been "sold a bill of goods" and that their A's were something of a fraud. At the end of her very discouraging first year, Lynn was faced with a difficult choice: call a halt to this charade of playing "college counselor" and go back to the classroom, or try to bring about change at the school.

After some deep soul searching and a quest for allies among her colleagues, Lynn settled on the latter course. She went to the principal and said she would like to propose something different—something that borrowed a few lessons from Millay's successes on the athletic field. At first, the principal wouldn't listen. But after he received a visit from a group of parents concerned about the academic program at Millay (a group formed at the instigation of Lynn and two of her colleagues), he relented and gave the trio 24 hours to come up with a plan. That night, the Millay College Core Curriculum (CCC) was born. The idea was actually quite simple. The program was based on the belief that every student has a right to be in a challenging program, and that the school has the responsibility to support all students' educational growth.

To start, Lynn and her colleagues visited every class at Millay's feeder schools to invite and recruit incoming Millay students to participate in a new program especially designed for students who wanted to go to college. Eligibility for admission to the program was offered to all students who expressed a desire to go to college, regardless of grade-point average or other measures of ability. Their past performance was irrelevant; what mattered was that the students wanted to attend college and were willing to put forth the effort to achieve that goal. After some cajoling and encouragement, 200 students signed up for the program in its first year (compared to the 30 who had participated in honors courses in the previous year). Six teachers participated in the new college-preparatory program that balanced high expectations with high levels of support.

Although students (and their parents or guardians) had signed a contract stipulating that they wanted to attend college and would maintain good study habits, their behavior did not change overnight. The students needed to learn what "college-bound behavior" was, and they needed to practice such behavior regularly. In other words, the students needed a considerable amount of counseling and guidance.

Lynn began to play a significantly different role from that of the traditional high school counselor. She became proactive in ensuring that students met the program's expectations (e.g., completed their homework, studied for exams, or signed up for the PSAT/NMSQT). This involved teaching students basic study habits and helping them understand the relationship of these study habits to their aspiration to attend college. She became an advocate for students with teachers and administrators. Rather than excluding from the program students who were not successful initially, she tried instead to identify the barriers to students' achievement and to design interventions to remove these barriers. She also needed to fill gaps in students' knowledge about college.

For example, only 40 of the first cohort of 200 students signed up to take the PSAT/NMSQT. Rather than accept the conclusion that "these students aren't interested in going to college after all," Lynn talked to the students directly and discovered that they didn't understand what the exam was or why they needed to take it. The next time around, almost all the CCC students signed up for the test, and currently, approximately 500 students take the PSAT/NMSQT each year, making Millay's the second highest test-taking population in the Los Angeles Unified School District.

In the program's second year, 270 students signed up for the CCC, and by the third year, one third of the Millay student body (1,100 students) was participating in the program. The growing popularity of CCC created some new challenges for Lynn and her colleagues. First, students continued to need counseling for personal problems and crises, including pregnancy, drug use, and family violence. As a counselor, Lynn knew these students needed prompt attention, but she lacked the time to spend in individual counseling with each student in need. The solution was to develop a strong network of social service agencies throughout the community. Lynn would provide immediate crisis intervention services, and refer students to another appropriate service provider. She would follow up on the referrals to ensure that the students' needs were met and to communicate her caring and concern, but she reserved most of her time for academic guidance and counseling activities.

A second challenge was that, as students enrolled in more Advanced Placement (AP) courses, the costs of these tests became prohibitive for students from low income families. The CCC staff also wanted to offer rewards and incentives to students for high achievement, but did not have the means to do so. A solution was found through the creation of an academic booster club. Parents and community members in the booster clubs raised money to help students meet the costs of taking AP tests, to provide rewards and recognition for high achievement, and to build community support for academic achievement.

Since CCC began in 1978, student achievement at Millay High School has increased dramatically. Before CCC, only 15 percent of Millay graduates enrolled in college, and those who did tended to enroll in community colleges or California state universities. Now about 70 percent of graduates go on to any of 80 different colleges and universities nationwide, including such elite institutions such as Stanford, Harvard, Spelman, and the University of California. By 1986, Millay sent more minority students to the University of California than did any other of the 49 high schools in the Los Angeles Unified School District. Scholarship support for Millay High School students has increased from $500,000 to $2.8 million in slightly over a decade.

A study conducted by the California Postsecondary Education Commission (1982) showed that students from Millay High School were succeeding in college. The study showed that the differential between students' grade-point averages in high school and those they achieved in college was declining. The CCC not only helped students gain access to college, but also helped them remain in college and achieve at high levels in postsecondary study.

In 1992, Millay High School graduated its thirteenth cohort of CCC students. Over this time, the program has grown from 6 to 60 teachers and from 1 to 12 AP courses (with a 68 percent passing rate). Additional science, math, and language classes, including some that were never offered before, have been added to the curriculum. Eight colleges and universities work with Millay in partnerships to improve students' education and provide exposure to college campuses.

Lynn and the two other people who started the CCC are no longer working at Millay High School. The principal who first allowed them to begin the program has also moved on. But the program continues because it has become institutionalized. It is part of school culture, and staff, students, and community members expect it to continue. What began as a dream shared by a few people is now part of what Millay does on a regular basis.

Lynn's experience demonstrates the potential for school counselors to become leaders in education reform. By believing in students' capacity for achievement and accepting the responsibility to help them develop this capacity, a small team was able to create organizational changes at Millay High that resulted in greatly improved educational processes and outcomes, including a revitalized faculty and staff, a student body that valued academic achievement and achieved at high levels, and a community that supported the students' efforts and aspirations.

Positive Effects

That counselors' efforts may have a positive effect on students is amply demonstrated by the following case histories drawn from Millay High School's CCC.

Manuel

Manuel's parents are farm workers with no more than a third-grade education. He was enrolled in English-as-a-second-language classes in junior high school, but when he signed up for the CCC, he just took off academically. By the time he was a senior, he was taking five Advanced Placement courses, and he received a score of 5 on each of the exams. He entered Occidental College in Los Angeles as a sophomore. His guidance counselor received the following letter from one of Manuel's college professors, in calculus, no less: "Thank you for sending us Manuel. In 17 years of teaching, I've never had a finer student." Without the CCC, this student would not have gone to college. He is now an engineer and has finished not only Occidental College but also graduate work at Stanford University.

Lisa

The second student, Lisa, came from an abusive home. She had no parental support and was tossed back and forth from place to place. Before she left for college, Lisa told her guidance counselor, "When you came to the junior high and talked to us about going to college, I felt pushed to sign that contract. I never really believed that I was bright until this year, as a senior, after we read a novel in AP English. When we finished reading the novel and writing the paper, and I got a good grade with good comments, I looked back at the book and saw stamped there 'For gifted students only.' It was at that moment I realized I could do the work."

Walter

Walter is a virtual archetype of what is happening to black males in this country. He was the kind of guy for whom football was the highest priority, and schoolwork came much further down the list. Walter signed up for the CCC because he wanted to attend the University of California at Berkeley, but he also wanted to play high school football. He asked to take the minimum number of college-preparatory courses, just enough to be admitted to college. If he continued on this road, he might get admitted to Berkeley but probably wouldn't finish. His guidance counselor conspired with Walter's parents, deciding that it would be a good experience for Walter to go to a prep school in the summer to experience a challenging academic program. He was accepted to the summer session at Andover with a scholarship. After one grueling summer, he came home a convert and said, "Put me in those AP classes. If this is anything like Berkeley, I'd better do more than the minimum."

Walter was admitted to Berkeley as a special-action student. When he left for college, his guidance counselor told him, "Remember to send me your college graduation announcement, because I do expect you to graduate." Not only did Walter send the announcement, he also went on to medical school and will soon be finishing.

Lolita

The first black student Millay sent to Princeton was a young woman named Lolita. She was the kind of student teachers either loved or hated to have in their class — she challenged them often and asked lots of questions. When the Princeton representative came to campus, Lolita was called to the guidance office as the perfect candidate. After she applied to a number of colleges and was accepted to all of them, she did indeed choose Princeton. She recounts this story from her freshman year:

> The other day, I went to a tea given by the Class of 1932, and they asked us how it was that we ended up at Princeton. The first student said that her father was a Yale graduate and her mother was a Princeton graduate, so her parents argued from the time she was a child about where she should go, and her choice of Princeton caused a big family conflict. The second student pointed to a dining hall down the way and announced that it had been named after his great-grandfather, so he had always known he would go to to Princeton. When it was my turn, I told them that to be very honest, I hadn't even heard of Princeton until my senior year in high school. Those ladies were in shock. Their teacups rattled in their saucers.

Not surprisingly, Lolita has since graduated from Princeton. She went to law school and is now an attorney.

Debra

Debra is the kind of student who most frustrates guidance counselors. Debra had about 2,000 conferences with her counselor during her three years at Millay and every time the issue was the same—Debra was not doing her homework and was receiving D's and F's on her report card. Each time, she would promise to do better, but she rarely followed through. Although she wanted to stay in the CCC, she was reducing her options concerning going to college and might not even graduate from high school on time.

Debra looked back on her last counseling session, where her counselor pointed out her grade-point average of 1.6 and told her that her only option was to go to the community college. "I went to community college, grew up a lot, and decided to study. I transferred to Cal State Long Beach, graduated with honors, and now I'm at UC Irvine, working with junior high school students just like I was to help them believe they can go to college, too."

3

The Counseling Profession

Ruth, Richard, and Lynn, discussed in the previous chapter, are three of the nation's approximately 70,000 school counselors. Together, they represent about 1.7 percent of public school personnel nationwide, although the portion varies from state to state.

Although complete information is not available, data based on a 1991 survey of AACD membership suggest that about two-thirds of counselors are female and about 90 percent are non-Hispanic whites. Over one-fifth (23 percent) report receiving salaries below $20,000 per year; 30 percent earned between $20,000 and $29,999; while 22 percent earned between $30,000 and $39,999; and 24 percent earned $40,000 or more. Tables 1 and 2 in the Appendix contain summary data on the counseling profession.

The career ladder for counselors is typically quite limited. Many counselors begin their careers as teachers. After entering counseling, they can aspire to become counseling directors, but relatively few counselors either move into administrative positions or return voluntarily to the classroom. Thus, most counselors remain in the profession for most of their careers.

Tenure policies vary by state and district. In many districts, counselors enter the field through teaching. After several years of teaching, they can request assignment as counselors, provided they have received a state counseling credential. Under these conditions, counselors often have tenure as teachers. That is, they serve as counselors at the discretion of their principals, but can return to the classroom if removed from counseling duty. In practice, however, few principals use their discretionary authority to remove counselors from their positions. In other districts, counselors enter the field directly following graduate training and credentialing, with no requirements for teaching experience. Under these conditions, some districts offer tenure to counselors and some do not.

Access to Counseling

Estimates of the ratio of school counselors to students vary. Department of Education statistics indicate a national ratio of 551 students for every counselor (National Center for Education Statistics, 1990). However, the ratio varies considerably from school to school.

The number of students per counselor is increasing in many areas of the country. The Commission on Precollege Guidance and Counseling describes increasing counselor-student ratios in some states (1986a, p. 16). In some areas of California, counselors who used to advise 250 students now have caseloads twice or three times that size. In the Los Angeles Unified School District, the second largest school district in the nation, the counselor-student ratio is now 1:650 at the high school level and 1:1,000 at the middle school level.

Current counselor-student ratios are far higher than what is recommended by professional associations. Both the American School Counselor Association (ASCA) and NACAC recommend ratios between 1:100 (considered ideal) and 1:300 (considered the maximum acceptable ratio).

In 1988, ASCA adopted the following position:

> It is the position of the American School Counselor Association that the counselor-student ratio be determined by considering the major factor of student growth and development. It is recommended that school districts implement the goals and objectives of a comprehensive and developmental guidance program for students at all levels, kindergarten through postsecondary. To implement such a program, additional factors such as guidance and counseling program scope, role, function and job description of the school counselor, the number of instructional staff as well as the support staff available to the educational process must be considered. While published reports such as *High School* by Ernest Boyer recommend ideal counselor-student ratios of 1:100, ASCA is aware that each school district is unique; what may be an ideal caseload in one school district may be untenable in others. ASCA maintains that implementation of a comprehensive guidance and counselor program meeting the developmental needs of students be the primary determinant, and that the recommended ratio be between 1:100 (ideal) and 1:300 (maximum). (ASCA 1988)

In general, students from low-income families, students of color, and students in both rural and inner-city areas are most likely to attend schools with high counselor-student ratios. Lee and Ekstrom (1987) summarized their analysis of comprehensive national data as follows:

> We find that students without such access are more likely to be disadvantaged—in terms of both social class and minority status. Thus, the lack of counseling at high school entry is particularly concentrated [among] students who are least likely to be able to turn to their families as an alternative or supplemental source of information in these matters. The fact that disadvantaged, rural, and minority students are less likely to receive program planning counseling than are their more advantaged and white counterparts implies that students who need good advice the most probably get it the least. (p. 306)

Access to counseling may be most limited in some rural areas, where, according to the National Vocational Guidance Association, over 90 percent of the children lack any access to guidance programs. Access to counseling also varies across grade levels. The counselor-student ratio in elementary schools is estimated to be between 1:700 and 1:1,000 (Bobele and Conran 1988), with large numbers of elementary school children lacking any access to guidance programs. The scarcity of educational counseling in elementary and middle schools is particularly troublesome because students face critical points in their educational development throughout this period. In the elementary years, for example, third grade emerges as a critical point at which differences in achievement among children become amplified and many children who have been labeled as having low ability begin to lose motivation. Middle school is also critical because students at this point are first segregated into tracks and assigned to courses that will later determine their eligibility for college admission. The availability of counseling often shows an inverse relationship to the demonstrated need for counseling; in general, those with the most need have the least access (Lee and Ekstrom 1987).

Outcomes of Counseling

Although the ratio of students to counselors provides an indicator of student access to guidance and counseling services in the schools, a more important question is how access to counseling influences students' education and achievement. According to the Commission on Precollege Guidance and Counseling, "Since many of the outcomes of guidance and counseling programs are not easily quantified, it is difficult to. demonstrate success or to show the risk to students if they do not get the services" (1986a, p. 16).

Controlled studies on counseling outcomes are scarce, but there are some clues in various analyses of national *High School and Beyond* survey data. These findings typically indicate a correlation between greater access to counseling and higher levels of achievement. Students with less access to counseling are "more likely to be placed in nonacademic tracks and to take fewer math courses" (Moles 1991, p. 164). Students reporting access to counseling were significantly more likely to be placed in an academic track, rather than a general curriculum or a vocational track (Lee and Ekstrom 1987).

Additional analyses support the effectiveness of counseling for middle school students. For example, Mayer's (1991) evaluation of early awareness programs provided to middle school and early high school students concluded that schools offering such programs help to narrow the gap between students' aspirations to attend college and the courses they take, which often do not prepare students for college.

Counseling Activities

One of the reasons that the outcomes of counseling remain vague and ill-defined is that counseling tends to be viewed more in terms of its processes than its effects. That is, both counselors themselves and the professional literature describe counseling by reference to the activities in which a counselor engages, rather than the effects of those activities upon the student or the school.

Typically counselors are called upon to play a wide variety of roles within the schools and have responsibility for a range of activities. The Commission on Precollege Guidance and Counseling (1986a) offered the following list of responsibilities (which they cautioned is not comprehensive):

> class scheduling and assigning students to courses; monitoring attendance; administering and interpreting tests; participating in and managing procedures for special education placements; assisting students in the college application and financial aid process; providing career information and guidance; working with and sometimes disciplining students who have been identified as having attitude or behavior problems; dealing with personal issues and crises from substance abuse to teenage pregnancy; acting as a liaison for the school with other social agencies serving children; and communicating with parents on a wide range of subjects. (pp. 13–14)

Similarly, Boyer (1988) described the role of the counselor as follows:

> Today in most high schools in the United States, counselors are not only expected to advise students about college, they are also asked to police for drugs, keep records of dropouts, reduce teenage pregnancy, check traffic in the halls, smooth the tempers of irate parents, and give aid and comfort to battered and neglected children. School counselors are expected to do what our communities, our homes, and our churches have not been able to accomplish, and if they cannot, we condemn them for failing to fulfill our high-minded expectations. (p. 3)

Perhaps due to these many responsibilities, the activities of most counselors reflect a reactive rather than a proactive approach. For example, most counselors assume that students who want to go to college will visit the school's college office to ask for assistance. Students who don't visit the college office are assumed to have little interest in attending college; therefore, the counselors seldom initiate contact to ascertain students' level of interest in attending college, to correct any inaccurate information or beliefs, and to encourage students to consider college. Similarly, most counselors assume that parents who don't come to school or contact the counselor are not interested in their children's education. The counselors therefore rarely take the initiative in contacting parents and inviting their participation or involvement.

This reactive approach is reflected in activities in which counselors generally do not engage. For example, they rarely:

- sit on curriculum committees or other major policymaking groups within the school;
- attend teacher training programs or other programs that concern learning theory or teaching methods;
- collect or disseminate information about student outcomes or provide consultation to teachers or administrators about student and institutional problems or needs;
- visit or evaluate social service agencies in the community that could provide assistance to students, or
- train teachers, students, or other staff to assist them in certain aspects of student guidance or counseling.

Each of these is an example of activities in which counselors would more often engage if they were guided by an underlying philosophy that emphasized the pivotal role of the counselor in enabling students to achieve at the highest possible levels.

Models of Counseling

Counseling activities are influenced by the prevailing models or para-
digms of counseling. Since school counseling first emerged as an educational function at the turn of the century, several different models
have guided practice. Gysbers and Henderson (1988) described a succes-
sion of models, ranging from early counseling programs that were
exclusively vocational in orientation to those that emphasize guidance,
assessment, and psychological counseling. Most recently, what are
known as comprehensive developmental models focus on healthy development in many areas of life.

Comprehensive developmental models of counseling are endorsed
by ASCA and form the foundation for many of the state plans developed
over the last decade. These models emerged in response to concerns
that counseling was focusing on psychologically troubled students to
the exclusion of those experiencing "normal" development and growing
interest in career development theory and systems theory.

Gysbers and Henderson (1988) listed three key components of the
comprehensive developmental model:

> First, guidance is a program. As a program it has characteristics
> similar to [those of] other programs in education, including: (1)
> student outcomes (student competencies); (2) activities and pro-
> cesses to assist students in achieving these outcomes; (3) profes-
> sionally recognized personnel; and (4) materials and resources. Sec-
> ond, guidance programs are developmental and comprehensive.
> They are developmental in that guidance activities are conducted
> on a regular and planned basis to assist students to achieve specified
> competencies. . . . Guidance programs are comprehensive in that a
> full range of activities and services such as assessment, information,
> consultation, counseling, referral, placement, follow-up, and follow-
> through are provided. Third, guidance programs feature a team
> approach. A comprehensive, developmental program of guidance
> is based on the assumption that all school staff are involved. At the
> same time, it is understood that professionally certified school coun-
> selors are central to the program. (pp. 30–31)

Plans drawn up for Wisconsin and Missouri provide examples of
how states have used this approach. The Wisconsin model is organized
around student competencies, such as "learning to learn" (educational
skills and competencies); "learning to live" (life skills); and "learning
to work" (career planning and work skills). The Missouri model, in
contrast, is organized around program components including: (1) guidance curriculum (using a classroom or small-group setting to teach

particular competencies to students); (2) individual planning and advising (students and counselors meeting one-on-one): (3) responsive services (both preventive and remedial interventions for those students facing problems that interfere with their well-being and development); and (4) system support (e.g., staff development, evaluation, public relations, administrative duties, and other functions needed to accomplish the aims of the program).

Counseling plans based on comprehensive developmental models have many strengths. Among these are their emphasis on a team approach to counseling that involves teachers, parents, and community members; and provision of services to all students, rather than concentrating primarily on troubled students. In addition, the models recognize the importance of providing counseling from the elementary years through twelfth grade. The comprehensive developmental approach asserts that counseling is an integral aspect, not a supplemental service, of education at the elementary and secondary levels. Further, the models attempt to specify counselors' goals and responsibilities more clearly than has been done before. They also attempt to increase counselors' accountability by providing objective evaluation standards.

On the other hand, the comprehensive developmental models have several weaknesses. A primary concern is that, in attempting to address the developmental needs of students in a broad and comprehensive manner, many of the counseling programs based on these models do not clearly establish the primacy of student academic achievement in their goal statements and activities. Rather, most comprehensive developmental plans stress the acquisition of particular student competencies that include, but do not necessarily emphasize, achievement. It is implicit in the comprehensive developmental models that the mastery of student competencies will promote academic success, and adherents of these models argue that the ultimate goal is to improve students' learning and achievement. However, this point often is not evident in written plans and program descriptions.

Many of the goal statements for school counseling and guidance based on the comprehensive developmental models are vague and linked only indirectly to achievement. For example, in 1987 the California State Department of Education established the following counseling goals in state standards for comprehensive developmental guidance programs:

> (1) Students acquire regular and timely information to enable them to make informed decisions; (2) Students develop self-management and planning skills; (3) Students are assisted in overcoming disa-

bling educational/personal/social problems; and (4) Students experience a supportive and rewarding learning environment. (California State Department of Education, cited in Gysbers and Henderson 1988, p. 29)

A second and related concern is that the comprehensive developmental models do not consistently hold counselors accountable for contributing to academic success and achievement for all students (as measured by grades, courses in which students enroll, graduation rates, college admission, or other measurable indicators). In theory, the development of student competencies should promote academic success, but the accountability and evaluation processes used in the comprehensive developmental models often fail to assess the degree to which this actually occurs. As a result, counselors can become focused on assisting students to develop specific competencies without regard for the degree to which these competencies result in higher achievement, graduation and college admission rates, lower dropout rates, or other indicators of academic success.

A third concern about the comprehensive developmental models is the degree to which they are actually being implemented in the schools. Although comprehensive developmental approaches have produced a number of elegant and elaborate plans at the state or district level, observation suggests that implementation is uneven.

4

How Counselors Are Trained

There are nearly 600 institutions in the United States that provide undergraduate or graduate training in school counseling. Many programs are located within schools or colleges of education, but some are in psychology departments. Together, they award about 4,000 master's degrees, 300 doctoral degrees, and an indeterminate number of bachelor's degrees in school counseling every year. (The figures for the latter are uncertain in that undergraduate degrees may lead to careers in a variety of counseling professions above and beyond school counseling.) Most states require the equivalent of a master's degree plus a teaching certificate or a year of practical experience for counselor certification. Counselors may also seek national certification from the National Board of Certified Counselors (NBCC).

In the field of counseling, the Council for Accreditation of Counseling and Related Educational Programs (CACREP), an affiliate of the American Association of Counseling and Development (AACD) established accreditation standards in 1981 and is generally recognized as the principal accrediting agency. CACREP standards are concerned with program content, faculty quality, and supervised experience (Herr 1986). Students must complete course work in human growth and development, social and cultural foundations of our society, helping relationships, groups, lifestyle and career development, research and evaluation, and professional orientation.

There are two benefits of graduation from a CACREP program. First, graduates can more quickly and easily qualify to take one of the exams developed by independent certifying agencies (e.g., NBCC and the National Academy for Certified Clinical Mental Health Counselors). For example, NBCC allows graduates of CACREP programs to sit for its examination immediately upon graduation, while graduates of non-CACREP programs must first have two years of postgraduate supervision. Second, some states, such as Virginia and Maryland, will certify graduates of CACREP programs upon graduation. Other states give preference in hiring to CACREP graduates. But in many states, neither graduation from a CACREP-accredited institution nor certification through passing an examination is necessary to function as a school counselor.

Currently, only 62 institutions—or one-tenth of the total offering counseling programs—have earned CACREP accreditation. The majority of school counselors do not receive training in CACREP-accredited institutions. Consequently, the quality of their training varies widely. Some have completed lengthy, high-quality, intellectually rigorous programs, while others have had only low-level instruction over a short period of time. (See Appendixes A and B for additional information about counselor education)

In-Service Training

In reality, most counselors learn on the job. They pick up some skills during informal orientation the week before school starts and some from "in-service training" during the school year. But mostly they "learn by doing" through old-fashioned trial and error. The orientation session is a key meeting in which, directly or indirectly, incoming counselors learn about the school's educational philosophy, expectations regarding the counselor's role and activities, and standards for job performance. The typical orientation meeting does little, however, to provide a conceptual foundation and set high standards for job performance. Instead, new counselors are often presented with a bewildering array of policies and procedures. One state, for example, provides counselors with a thick binder containing materials ranging from statistical tables about dropouts to a catalog of career-assessment instruments and a state association proposal for guidance reform. It is hard to imagine an incoming counselor deriving a clear sense of purpose and direction from such a compilation.

Unfortunately, in-service training is rarely much better. According to Herr (1986):

> While many school districts have a day or so mandated each year
> to be devoted to in-service training of school counselors or teachers,

the content of such training is frequently not based on needs assessment or analyses of the competencies counselors must have in order to discharge their responsibilities most effectively. Many in-service programs are not designed to develop specific skill sets in counselors. Instead, they tend to be one-shot, brief exposures to a topical area of concern in a particular district at a particular time. (p. 15)

A typical in-service meeting is held at the end of a long school day, in a dingy meeting room in the district office. During the meeting, a bored administrator reads aloud a number of announcements and bulletins and introduces a few guest speakers who make brief presentations. These events typically vary widely in content and show little, if any, connection to one another. For example, one agenda might include child abuse reporting procedures, new scholarships for handicapped students, military testing dates, and deadlines for registering for the PSAT/NMSQT. Following the announcements (or possibly even at the same time), counselors might also be asked to complete some forms.

The very manner in which most in-service meetings are conducted devalues the activity and reduces its professionalism. The separation of counselors' in-service training from that for teachers reinforces the perception that school counseling is an ancillary component of the education process. Of most concern, however, is that the typical in-service meeting is in no way connected to goals or outcomes related to student achievement.

Professional Associations

Professional associations serving school counselors are a major resource for training and development, through both publications and programs. ASCA, a division of the American Association for Counseling and Development, is the association serving the profession most directly and has more than 12,500 members. In addition to conferences, professional development programs, and advocacy activities, ASCA publishes several journals and newsletters including *The School Counselor, Elementary School Guidance and Counseling*, the *ASCA Counselor*, and the *ASCA Newsletter*. In addition, every state except Vermont has a statewide school counselor association. The state associations function autonomously, but their by-laws and codes of ethics must be consistent with those of the national organization.

Several other associations provide services to the field. Some of these are also part of AACD, including the Association for Counselor Education and Supervision (ACES), the American Rehabilitation Counseling Association, the Association for Humanistic Education and Development, and the National Career Development Association. A significant number of school counselors also belong to NACAC.

Although professional associations are influential in policy development, their impact on the day-to-day lives of school counselors is mixed. They can contribute a great deal to those counselors who can meet the costs of membership and registration for conferences and workshops, who are motivated to attend, and who approach their work with a sense of professionalism. Once again, however, the counselors most in need of external support—namely those in low-income school districts who are besieged by responsibilities and problems and who may have lost their belief in their own ability to make a difference in the lives of students—typically get less support from professional associations because they are less likely to be members. Such counselors may lack the resources to attend association events, but feelings of isolation, alienation, shame at the condition of their schools, or hopelessness may also deter their participation.

Continuing Professional Development

Most counselors participate in some continuing professional development activities, usually sponsored by professional associations, but sometimes sponsored by local colleges or universities or other nonprofit agencies. The quality and usefulness of these sessions vary greatly.

ASCA offers different kinds of professional development opportunities. On a national level, it offers professional development institutes throughout the country. In addition, the ASCA leadership conference (attended by leaders of the state associations) usually includes workshops for participants, with the goal of training these participants to then deliver the workshops to other counselors in their states. In 1991, four workshops were offered, with supporting materials made available to participants.

In addition to ASCA workshops, school counselors can attend meetings of other professional associations, such as the College Board, the American College Testing Program (ACT), NACAC, or individual state school counselor associations. Exact numbers are not available, but it is safe to say that relatively few counselors attend these meetings. Those who do attend usually represent affluent school districts that already offer strong educational and counseling programs. Thus, the counselors most in need of such training and information (usually from inner-city or rural school districts) are probably least likely to attend, partly because the costs are prohibitive.

Professional conferences provide useful information to help counselors refine their skills for assisting the college-bound population. However, relatively few of them challenge counselors to exercise the same level of skill and caring for students who are not in precollege programs and they seldom address the equity issues confronting the education system.

5

Six Major Problems in School Counseling

Our analysis points to six major problems that constrain the effectiveness of school counseling and guidance.

Lack of Basic Philosophy

Few counselors are guided by a well-developed philosophy of their roles and goals. Few counselors are guided in their work by a belief system that clearly spells out their goals and values. Without such background, they cannot independently establish priorities, advocate effectively for change, or approach their work in a proactive manner. Instead, counselors become reactive, responding to the priorities or needs established by others, and accepting the role of ancillary or support staff. Such counselors will have difficulty justifying their activities and will be more likely to be assigned (and to accept) nonprofessional, quasi-administrative duties.

Because many counselors lack this philosophical foundation, they too often lose sight of the fact that their primary goal should be to assist students in learning and achieving in school. "The counselor must keep in mind that the ultimate goal of the school is academic success. All other services are focused toward enhancing that goal" (Hannaford 1987, p. 7; cf., Burtnett 1988). Yet, in practice, many schools fail to facilitate or enable students' academic success, and too often counselors conform to the beliefs and attitudes that prevail in the school and that constrain academic success.

Because many counselors lack a philosophical base of their own, they more easily accept the prevailing philosophy of the school. They may come to believe that certain groups of students (usually poor and minority students) are incapable, lack potential or ability, and are best placed in remedial courses or vocational tracks. They may accept the view that students' self-esteem will be strengthened if the counselor protects them from challenges rather than encouraging them to accept challenges. Or they may accept the view that the school is helpless and unable to improve student achievement and learning.

Counselors also need to believe in their ability to be effective agents for change. This requires that they receive training in organizational skills, but it also requires the willingness and confidence to be out in front of the change process. All too often, counselors (and others) feel unwilling or unable to effect meaningful change until someone else (e.g., the state, school board, principal, or students themselves) takes action. Although such actions may be highly desirable, they should not be a prerequisite for effective action on the counselor's part.

Poor Integration

Counseling remains an ancillary, rather than a core, component of K through 12 education. Few schools have recognized or developed the unique potential of school counseling to strengthen elementary and secondary education. Despite the fact that counselors are in an excellent position to observe the effects of school policy and practice on student achievement, counseling and teaching are for the most part poorly integrated or coordinated. Counselors have little influence over curriculum development and other kinds of decision making within the school. For example, few schools include counselors on their curriculum committees, and many teachers express ignorance of the counselor's daily activities. Further, few counselors have a thorough understanding of their school's curriculum, and even fewer are knowledgeable about research and practice concerning teaching methods, curriculum development, learning styles, or school reform. Only infrequently do counselors attempt to describe their role and accomplishments to others within the school.

The result is that counselors lose the opportunity to serve as leaders and agents of change in promoting school improvement and student achievement. The information and feedback they are capable of providing, based on their interactions with a broad cross section of students and teachers, are infrequently expressed and typically undervalued by administrators, teachers, and even the counselors themselves. Further, the attitude that counseling is a support service of secondary importance to the education process makes it easier for administrators to assign counselors additional, nonprofessional duties.

It is important to note that counselors must be taught how to bring about change. Simply suggesting that they do so, without teaching them the skills required, giving them a conceptual foundation, and changing the attitudes of teachers and administrators is unlikely to have positive effects on students, schools, or counselors. The continued status of counseling as an ancillary service reflects, to some extent, gaps in graduate and professional training of all educators.

Insufficient Student Access

The typical high counselor-student ratios indicate that few counselors have the time to adequately serve all the students assigned to them. For example, given the ratio of 1:650 in the Los Angeles Unified School District high schools, counselors are simply unable to offer individual guidance to each student concerning their educational programs and career goals.

This problem is exacerbated because, for a variety of reasons, counselors are often called upon to provide general kinds of administrative support in addition to their professional responsibilities (Gysbers and Henderson 1988). The large number of such nonprofessional duties assigned to counselors suggests that their role is poorly defined and earns little respect from school administrators. Thus, rather than simply exhorting teachers and administrators to relieve them of such duties, counselors must clarify their role for others and demonstrate that it is in the best interests of the students and the school for the counselors to be engaged in guidance and counseling-related activities on a full-time basis.

Student access to educational guidance is further limited when counselors spend most of their time providing individual therapy to students with emotional or behavioral problems. Many counselors receive psychologically oriented training and, many, although not all, are most comfortable with psychological counseling. Further, the students they serve face many serious problems for which counseling would be indicated (e.g., drug abuse, teen pregnancy, family violence). Although assisting students with such problems is an essential aspect of the counselor's role, the proportion of time devoted to this activity may have to be changed. Because most counselors are responsible for serving hundreds of students, they simply do not have the time to provide extensive individual counseling to those students in need, while simultaneously providing educational guidance to others. Increasing the number of counselors in the schools may be helpful or even necessary in improving school counseling, but these steps are not sufficient. Without a major shift in the activities and philosophy of school counselors, simply increasing their numbers will do little to improve student achievement. High counselor-student ratios require that counselors examine and revise their traditional approach to their jobs (see Herr 1991; NASFAA and ACE 1989).

Inadequate Guidance of Some Students

Low-income and minority students typically get shortchanged because they have less access to counselors than do other students, especially for help in educational guidance. Counselor-student ratios are especially high in inner-city schools, and few students in these schools have the opportunity to obtain information, encouragement, and guidance about their educational programs. Unfortunately, the students with the least access to counseling may have the greatest need for it. Herr (1991) wrote:

> Poor children are likely to have more intense needs for information, modeling, and mentoring. And certainly the parents of children from lower socioeconomic backgrounds need more and different support from the community and school than is true of families who are able to pay for private tutorial or guidance services if the school is unable to provide all that they desire. (p. 9)

In their role as gatekeepers, counselors are likely to deny low-income and minority students access to a rigorous academic curriculum and are more likely to direct them to general, vocational, or remedial curricula (NASFAA and ACE 1989). Thus, counselors contribute to the perpetuation of educational and societal inequities.

Because their families are often relatively unfamiliar with education policies and practices, low-income and minority students, are likely to have many misconceptions about the education system. They may believe that only rich kids go to college or that a straight-A average is required for college admission. They may aspire to careers that require a college degree but may not understand that if they do not take algebra in the eighth or ninth grade, they may not be eligible to attend college. When counselors fail to explore students' dreams, aspirations, and beliefs about the education system, they are passively contributing to continued inequity in education.

Finally, few counselors receive training in special issues related to minority students. Thus, counselors may be less effective in counseling such students and may inadvertently perpetuate negative stereotypes or self-fulfilling prophecies that hinder achievement.

Lack of Counselor Accountability

Student outcomes, especially the college-going rates of low-income, minority, and first-generation college students, are inadequate and unacceptable; dropout rates in urban inner-city schools are too high; and student achievement (e.g., performance on standardized tests) is too low. Schools in general, counselors included, are not doing their jobs.

Yet few educators, including counselors, are consistently held accountable for outcomes related to student achievement. In general, counselors are accountable for processes rather than outcomes. That is, they are typically evaluated on the basis of the number of activities or programs they conduct, the number of students they see, and the timeliness and accuracy of the paperwork they must produce. At best, counselors are held accountable for enrolling students in the classes needed to meet minimum requirements for high school graduation. For the most part, counselors are not evaluated on the basis of results, especially outcomes such as the number of students who enroll in precollege curricula, take the PSAT/NMSQT or SAT, graduate from high school, apply to college, or are accepted by a college. They are even less likely to be held accountable for how these results differ as a function of such student characteristics as race, gender, or ethnicity. They are rarely, if ever, held accountable for using information about student outcomes to take aggressive action to improve achievement for students who have less knowledge about college and how to get there.

This does not mean that counselors alone are accountable for student achievement. Ideally, every staff member in the school shares responsibility for promoting students' academic success. Unfortunately, the reality often is that no one is held accountable for the quality and outcomes of the education process.

Failure to Utilize Other Resources

Guidance and counseling are too often the exclusive domain of the school counselor(s), not the responsibility of the entire school. High counselor-student ratios, combined with the great need for support services among middle and secondary school students, suggest that guidance and counseling can no longer be provided exclusively by school counselors. To meet students' needs, teachers, administrators, parents, and community members must assume more responsibility for counseling and guidance. Tradition and territoriality combine to limit the extent to which this occurs in most schools.

Rather than continuing to accept exclusive responsibility for meeting students' guidance and counseling needs, counselors must learn to make use of other school and community services and create a network to which students can be referred for a variety of needs. From this perspective, counseling and guidance should connote a schoolwide and communitywide effort to meet student needs, with designated school counselors at its hub. This requires a level of communication and cooperation among school counselors, other school personnel, and the community at large that is not often seen today.

6

Toward a New Vision
of Counseling

In one suburban Los Angeles high school, almost half the student population consists of students of color who are bused in from various parts of the metropolitan area, but only one Hispanic student is enrolled in an Advanced Placement course. Across town in an inner-city high school, only a handful of students each year attain eligibility for admission to the University of California, and for several years, no students have actually attended a four-year college following their high school graduation. Neither school considers its situation to be an institutional problem. Teachers and administrators in the suburban school are vaguely aware of the disparity in student outcomes by ethnicity, but attribute it to differences in elementary education, family structure and values, and motivation. Some counseling staff feel that placing minority students in classes that may be too hard for them would counteract efforts to enhance their self-esteem. In the inner-city school, student outcomes are rarely if ever discussed in staff or faculty meetings.

In neither school is anyone standing up to say, "This is unacceptable. We can and must do better." In neither school is anyone challenging staff and faculty to improve students' achievement. In neither school do counselors, teachers, administrators, students, parents, or community members feel empowered to improve the quality of education. Neither principal has been asked by the district office to report information about student outcomes broken down by ethnicity and sex.

Neither district has been requested by the state to be accountable for achievement outcomes broken down by school and by ethnicity. No one is accountable for promoting high levels of student achievement. Rarely does anyone even take the time to study student outcomes and consider what they indicate about the quality of education the school provides.

Our vision for counseling cannot be separated from our vision for the education system overall. This nation needs schools to become places where every student is challenged and supported to achieve at the highest possible level. All of the resources of the school must be directed toward attaining this goal. Students should not be constrained by assignment to vocational or remedial tracks or by the assumptions of faculty and administration that some students have less ability than others. Rather, all students should be encouraged to seek out and accept challenges, and they should be supported and rewarded for doing so.

If this vision is realized, teachers and counselors will recognize that children learn in different ways and at different rates, and variation will not be used as a reason to doubt a child's potential or limit that child's opportunities to learn. Students' self-esteem will be fostered by encouraging them to accept challenges and helping them to achieve and meet rigorous academic demands, not by "protecting" them from challenge. In this way, the schools will strive to maximize each child's potential. Situations such as those described at the beginning of this chapter will be considered an affront to the community and to the children and will not be tolerated.

Given the state of public education today, we believe strongly that preparation for full participation in our society is best achieved through enrollment in a precollege curriculum. These curricula offer the greatest challenge and the most substance and are therefore most likely to prepare students to be productive members of society, whatever path they follow after high school. Based on our experience, we believe that even students who will not attend college will benefit from participation in a precollege curriculum, for they will learn to think and accept challenges and will acquire the discipline necessary to stick with even the toughest assignments. Therefore, even though some students will not choose college, we think it is most important to offer all students the opportunity to learn as if they were planning to attend college.

School guidance and counseling can contribute substantially in realizing this vision. To do so, however, counseling must change along the lines described below.

Belief in the Capacity of All Students to Learn

The National College Counseling Project (1986) stated, "Outstanding counselors . . . consistently emphasize that their students have the potential to better themselves and to meet ambitious goals" (p. 32). Counselors should be guided by an underlying philosophy that affirms the potential of each individual to achieve in school and successfully meet challenging academic demands. Thus, counselors should accept as their primary goal the responsibility for helping all students to achieve at the highest possible levels. They should encourage students to accept academic challenges and support students in their efforts to meet such challenges. Counselors should become advocates for students by acknowledging each student's potential for achievement and striving to remove institutional obstacles to that achievement. This approach is congruent with the recommendation of NASFAA and ACE (1989) that counseling programs should be built on the recognition that "all student groups, including minorities and other at-risk groups, have high aspirations and are capable of achieving in school" (p. 3).

Supporting students' achievement involves at least three broad components. First, counselors should provide emotional support by motivating and encouraging students to achieve at high levels, communicating their confidence in the students' abilities, and reassuring students if they do not successfully complete a course or an assignment that they still have the potential and capacity to achieve. Second, counselors should provide tangible support to students, by helping them acquire the skills and information they need to succeed. For example, a counselor may organize study groups, refer students to tutors, provide information about what courses they need to be eligible for college, or suggest particular courses that or teachers who might be especially helpful. Third, counselors should support student achievement by serving as the students' advocate within the school and intervening where necessary. For example, a counselor may point out to the principal recurring obstacles to student achievement, offer in-service programs to help teachers understand a variety of learning styles, meet individually with teachers who may be creating unnecessary obstacles to student learning and achievement, or encourage community members to support the school by serving as mentors or volunteers. The counselor should also refer students to internal and external resources and services as needed.

When counselors act from a philosophical foundation that affirms the capabilities of each individual, they will balance high expectations and high standards with high levels of support. The National College Counseling Project (1986) described excellent school counselors as follows:

> Students recognize these counselors as allies prepared to work energetically on their behalf. Without sacrificing the need for discipline and the "nagging" necessary to get some students to meet deadlines, the counselors have infused their work with an attitude of caring and support. (p. 32)

Assuming a Leadership Role

Once they have accepted the belief that all students can achieve at high levels, counselors can become a powerful force for school reform and education improvement. They can advocate that other members of the school community embrace their philosophy and accept the concomitant responsibility to help students maximize potential. Counselors can seek to identify institutional obstacles to learning and achievement, point out these obstacles to others in the school, and propose ways to overcome these obstacles. Counselors' contributions can be profound even when fairly simple actions are involved. For example, counselors in one Los Angeles middle school noted the high correlation between attendance and achievement in algebra; students who were often absent showed the lowest grades. In response, teachers were encouraged to call a student's home the first day that student was absent from class. This change in routine led to better attendance, and improved performance, in algebra classes.

Counselors are in a unique position to serve as agents of change. Because they see a large number of students who take a broad range of courses, counselors have a breadth of perspective that few if any other staff or faculty possess. (By contrast, teachers only observe students in the classes they teach, and administrators have a limited amount of direct contact with students.) Counselors have the opportunity to observe at first hand the effects of the school and the curriculum upon students; thus they have the responsibility to communicate and seek solutions to observed problems and shortcomings.

Being a leader also means reaching out to students and parents to invite their involvement in the learning process. When counselors reach out in this way, they teach students how to dream, to reach and strive for what may seem distant and unattainable. They can also explore students' and parents' beliefs about education, correct their misconceptions, and encourage them to revise their goals and aspirations in light of new information. They can help students translate their goals into actions, by explaining the connection between career and life goals and the choices made in school. A variety of analyses have pointed to large gaps in students' knowledge about their career and education options (see Rosenbaum 1976). For example, a California State Department of Education study (George 1989) found that 39 percent of tenth graders who reported an interest in attending college were not enrolled in the appropriate mathematics and science courses required to reach this goal. The counselor can and should play a key role in rectifying situations such as these.

In this way, the counselor can become the "academic conscience" of the school, ensuring that the school remains focused on student achievement and accepts responsibility for student outcomes. In so doing, the counselor will become a force for systemic change that permeates the entire school.

Coordination of Resources

In their efforts to promote achievement, school counselors should enlist support and aid. In this way, they can extend and improve the resources available to students, strengthen the school's and community's commitment to the counselor's philosophy, and relieve their burden of being the primary (or sole) direct service providers.

Counselors should train all school staff, from support staff through senior faculty and administrators, to contribute to the guidance function. For example, counselors could train teachers to conduct group sessions that provide students with basic information about precollege curricula. Individual sessions with counselors could be devoted to detailed and personalized guidance. Similarly, support staff could be trained to complete routine paperwork needed to enroll students in classes, so that counselors could use more of their time for advice and guidance. Such activities would have the additional benefit of uniting the school in its commitment to facilitating learning and achievement.

Students' psychological needs are crucial and must be met. Because individual counseling requires a substantial amount of time, however, counselors must use community resources more effectively. For example, counselors could develop referral networks of social service agencies and other community services. Counselors could provide limited crisis-intervention services and then refer students with continuing needs to outside agencies. Since these organizations might well specialize in the students' presenting problems, the students would receive better care, and the counselors would have the time to serve a broader range of students. In the process of developing this referral network, counselors would have the opportunity to explain their philosophies and beliefs to community members and thereby enlist support in promoting student achievement.

Counselors should also look to the community for support and assistance in their core mission of promoting student achievement. The value of using community resources for such a purpose has been widely recognized. For example, the National College Counseling Project (1986) discussed how partnerships with the business community can motivate students to achieve and continue their education by helping them learn about educational and career options. NASFAA and ACE (1989) described the merits of establishing alliances with local colleges and universities, particularly to strengthen students' early awareness of their options and to provide assistance with precollege advising and guidance. Herr (1991) has developed a model called "community guidance programs," in which partnerships between public school counselors, colleges and universities, businesses, other community organizations (e.g., civic organizations, religious groups), and parents are at the heart of the counseling process. Benefits include a community commitment to supporting student achievement; a broader range of resources and programs being made available to students, leading to improved student access to counseling; and more time for counselors to focus on academic counseling and guidance, rather than psychological counseling.

Counselor Accountability

Counselors and other school personnel are rarely held accountable for the results of their efforts. A new vision for counseling will hold all members of the school staff, including counselors, accountable for student achievement (see California State Department of Education 1990). A variety of indicators can be considered, including an ethnic breakdown of the number of students enrolling in particular courses; the number of students taking the PSAT/NMSQT or SAT exams; retention and graduation rates; and performance on standardized tests. When they are held accountable for such outcomes, all school personnel will be evaluated not on the basis of their activities, but rather on the basis of the results they obtain.

Counselors should also contribute to creating a climate of accountability within a school. Most counselors have access to considerable information about students: some is based on direct observation of students; some is anecdotal, based on feedback from students or school personnel; some comes from external sources, such as the state or

Educational Testing Service. For example, counselors can obtain information about enrollment patterns and course selections; the number of students taking the SAT or ACT and their scores; the number of college applications and the kinds of institutions to which they are submitted; the number of students accepted by colleges; students' college-going rates; and their grade-point averages in college. Such information enables the school to assess the levels of student achievement, celebrate its successes, and identify the challenges that remain. Breakdowns of various student subgroups (e.g., by ethnicity, race, gender) raise issues of equity. By disseminating this information to administrators, teachers, and even community members, the counselor can encourage reflection on the quality of existing education and indicate directions for change and improvement. Aggressive strategies may have to be developed to close the achievement gap—particularly for minority and poor students.

Dissemination of information alone is probably insufficient to promote positive change, however. In the absence of a conceptual framework that recognizes the responsibility of everyone in the school to promote student achievement, data can and will be interpreted in a manner that supports the status quo. For example, information that few graduates of an inner-city high school are successful in college can either provide an incentive for strengthening the precollege curriculum or be used to suggest that students attending the school shouldn't attempt college because they're sure to fail. Thus, the counselor should set a context for reviewing data and should also help others learn how to make use of such data.

Holding all school personnel accountable for student outcomes is important because it reflects the beliefs that the school is responsible for helping students achieve at the highest levels possible and that the school can make a difference in student achievement. This approach is contrary to many current accountability systems, which reinforce the belief that the school is powerless to influence student achievement.

7

Getting from Here to There: Implementing Needed Changes

There are three main strategies that would lead to better counseling and guidance:

1. Improving professional preparation and licensing requirements for school guidance counselors;
2. Improving in-service training of counselors and others involved in the guidance function;
3. Assisting schools to increase their overall achievement and college-going rates through more effective counseling and instruction and by meeting other student needs.

All three strategies need to be pursued. Our own bias, however, is toward a mixed strategy that includes the first two but emphasizes the third, because counseling and guidance are most likely to be permanently improved when they are viewed as central elements of a broader, whole-school effort to help all students achieve at the highest levels.

Improving Professional Preparation

On the average, counselors attend about five meetings of professional organizations, four meetings with employers, two meetings with community groups, and four "topical conferences" dealing with individual subjects germane to the field, during a single school year (Moles 1991). In addition, some try to keep up with developments in the field by subscribing to for example, the *Journal of Counseling and Development* (published by AACD) or to *The School Counselor* (from ASCA).

Is this preparation adequate to the purpose? The authors would like to see several changes in current counselor preparation, master's degree programs, continuing professional development programs, and in-service training.

Minimizing the Therapist Role

The first issue that warrants attention is the continuing emphasis on psychological counseling or therapy among school counselors, many of whom have been trained as mental health counselors. It is of course, essential that students receive counseling and support for their emotional, psychological, cognitive, or behavioral problems, because unmet needs in these areas will almost certainly interfere with a student's ability to learn and become successful. The issue is not whether students should have access to psychological counseling, but rather who should provide these services and how they should be provided.

Although many students have acute needs for psychological counseling, we question whether members of the school counseling staff should attempt to fill these needs. In our view, the effectiveness of school counseling would be increased if, rather than spending substantial amounts of time counseling a very small number of students, the counselors developed an excellent network of referrals throughout the community and directed students to the specialized resources needed. In this way, counselors could serve a broader range of students and would not be distracted from a primary emphasis on helping students achieve at high levels. Many counselors recognize the need to modify their practices in this area, but do not know how to do so.

To make such a change, counselors need training in how to:

- locate and evaluate potential referral sources;
- identify and contact community service agencies and determine if they would be appropriate and helpful for students;
- negotiate informal or formal agreements; and
- be effective advocates for students with external agencies.

Counselors also need training in administrative and management skills (see National College Counseling Project 1986) and lessons in how to make a good referral and how to follow it up.

Further, counselors need to learn to expand their referral networks by training others, inside and outside the schools, to provide guidance or counseling to students. This requires selecting individuals to join the network of service providers, designing and delivering a training program, and evaluating the skills of the trainees and their preparedness to provide guidance or counseling. Again, simply suggesting that counselors take these steps is insufficient to create long-lasting change; in addition, counselors must receive instruction in how to become effective coordinators.

Reducing Emphasis on Tracking

We are greatly concerned about the continuing emphasis on quantitative assessment in counselor training, with the goal of separating or grouping K through 12 students on the basis of perceived ability. As discussed earlier in this report, tracking and sorting generally have the effect of denying low-income and minority students, as well as many other students, access to the curricula and guidance they need to enter postsecondary education. Given the questionable predictive validity of the tests used for sorting and the devastating consequences for children of being placed in a vocational rather than a college-preparatory track, the appropriateness of continuing to train prospective counselors in these methods is questionable at best. To the extent that graduate schools, in-service training programs, and professional development programs support and train counselors to track students, they are directly contributing to educational inequities. A far better approach would be to emphasize the potential for achievement of each child, and to challenge school counselors to help the children develop this potential.

Increasing Training in Precollege Guidance

In reviewing counselor preparation standards developed or discussed by ASCA, CACREP, NBCC, state departments of education, and in the professional literature, Herr (1986) reported that little or no attention is paid to the counselor's role in advising and preparing students for college. Burtnett (1989) also contended that counselors need more training in precollege advising. His survey of counselor education programs indicated that only 4 out of 125 departments offered any courses in precollege guidance and counseling. The National College Counseling Project (1986) characterized counselor education in precollege advising as "haphazard" (p. 30). Thus, it is not surprising that counselors in practice often neglect this component of their role.

Focusing on Student Potential

Counselor education should stress that all students have the capacity to achieve at high levels and that the counselor's mission is to both challenge and support students so they can maximize their potential. To fulfill this mission, counselors must learn not only to provide emotional and tangible support directly to students (the traditional counseling role), but also how to contribute to the creation of a schoolwide environment that promotes student achievement.

The importance of conveying this philosophical base cannot be overemphasized. This philosophy will guide counselors in deciding how to spend their time, what responsibilities to accept, and what role to play within the school and community. It will add a sense of purpose and coherence to a role that often appears reactive and fragmented. It will empower the counselor to become an agent for change, if that is what is needed to help students learn.

Addressing Issues of Equity and Access

Training programs should describe how the education system perpetuates inequity and how counselors can begin to correct this situation. The programs should describe the factors that have shaped an "uneven academic playing field" on which low-income and minority students are disadvantaged. They should motivate, challenge, and prepare counselors to redress this situation.

Focusing on access and equity also means helping counselors become aware of and explore their own assumptions and beliefs. For example, data can be presented to challenge the common assumption that students who want to go to college know they must enroll in college-preparatory courses, and to demonstrate that few students actually succeed in moving from vocational or remedial tracks into general or precollege tracks. Instructors should also stimulate discussion about how to best foster students' self-esteem, and whether it is desirable for students to accept rigorous academic challenges even if they might fail.

Finally, focusing on access and equity also means conveying to counselors their responsibility to help shape a more even playing field. This requires counselors to be: aware of equity issues; able to recognize educational inequity where it occurs; and willing and able to take action to correct such situations. For example, counselors should be taught to compare student outcomes across ethnic groups, consider and investigate a variety of alternative explanations for observed differences among groups, and develop and implement interventions to reduce such differences.

Integrating Materials on Learning Styles and Teaching Methods

Because school counselors have a broad view of the school and interact with large numbers of students enrolled in diverse courses and programs, they are in a unique position to assess the effectiveness of the school in fostering achievement and to identify obstacles or barriers to high achievement. For this reason, counselors have much to contribute to decision making with regard to curriculum, staff development, school policy, and program development. To be an effective agent for change within the school, however, the counselor must be familiar with the language, theories, and practices of teaching and learning.

When counselors are educated about learning styles, they can help teachers recognize that different students learn in different ways and at different rates. When a student is having difficulty mastering course materials, a teacher might conclude that this student lacks ability and should move into a less challenging course. The counselor could gently challenge this conclusion by pointing out that the student has a different learning style and might respond to a modification in teaching methods. Counselors can convey this message either in one-on-one consultations with teachers about individual students or in group settings.

This recommendation also carries implications for staff development activities, such as in-service training sessions or continuing professional education. An understanding of teaching and learning theories on the part of those who instruct counselors would be beneficial. Knowledge of learning styles suggests that professional development is most effective when cooperative learning and experiential approaches are used, as opposed to "chalk and talk," conventional lecture sessions.

Improving Utilization of Data

A broad range of research and information from many different sources is available to counselors. Counselors should be informed about these resources and taught how to identify new sources of information. Further, they need skills in interpreting and understanding data. In particular, they should learn to relate quantitative information to policy and program issues (i.e., transform isolated bits of data into meaningful pieces of information). Toward this end, CACREP standards emphasize research and analysis skills.

Finally, counselors should learn to disseminate data and information and to help others in the school interpret them appropriately. When counselors are confident of their ability to transform raw data into useful information, they can help raise the consciousness of the entire school about student achievement and where improvements are needed.

Encouraging Leadership

Counselors need to learn about organizational behavior and development in order to become agents of change and leaders in school improvement. If counselors are to challenge the status quo, they need specific skills and a broad understanding of strategies for bringing about social change. When current training programs minimize these areas and instead stress quantitative sorting devices, future counselors get the message that they are not expected to "rock the boat."

Improving In-Service Training

The above-noted problems apply with equal force to in-service professional development activity. However, there are other features of in-service activity that also limit counselors' effectiveness. Many of these are structural, e.g., too little time is available; others involve problems with the way these programs are conceived. We have several suggestions for change.

- Even when only counselors are involved, professional development programs should place guidance and counseling activities within the broader context of an improvement effort that involves entire schools.
- Rather than beginning with a focus on guidance counselors—who they are, what they do, and what they need—counselor training programs should begin by asking what student outcomes we are trying to achieve and how guidance and counseling might contribute to these outcomes. Training stemming from this analysis would naturally try to improve the fit between institutional resources and students' needs for guidance and counseling (as a means of promoting achievement). School counselors may not necessarily be involved in the resulting interventions. In fact, teachers, community members, or others may be assigned considerable responsibility for these activities. An approach that focuses on the students and the school overall, rather than the counselors alone, may be more likely to lead to enduring improvements in student achievement.
- The most effective reforms balance short-term and long-term strategies for change. Short-term approaches typically supplement, extend, or enrich existing programs or curricula, without challenging the underlying philosophical and organizational structure. Mentoring programs, for example, supplement guidance and counseling by providing students with access to a caring and knowledgeable adult

who offers support and advice. Mentoring programs can lead to considerable improvements in student achievement, but they do not contribute to systemic change. If a mentoring program ended, student outcomes would probably revert to what they were before the programs were implemented. Long-term approaches, such as those implemented by the Achievement Council, a California nonprofit organization that works with schools and districts, promote lasting systemic change for minority and low-income students. The Achievement Council works with schools to develop organizational structures, accountability mechanisms, policies, and curricula that ensure a focus on student outcomes and student achievement. When the council withdraws its involvement, the school has internalized a change strategy and improvements in student achievement are maintained.

Both short- and long-term approaches are needed. Because long-term approaches require a considerable amount of time to implement, entire cohorts of students may receive inadequate education while the school is preparing for and slowly beginning the change process. Short-term approaches are crucial for meeting student needs during this time. While some programs do combine short- and long-term approaches, ordinarily a number of different programs are needed to provide this balance.

Helping Whole Schools

There is no easy prescription for implementing the vision described in the previous chapter. In the end, each school must undergo a rigorous process of self-examination to identify its strengths and needs and develop directions for change tailored to its unique environment. School staff and community members will have a larger stake in the success of their efforts if they are involved in the planning process. Whole-school reform activity is currently underway across the country. In a few cases, these activities were launched by individual school districts. More often, however, the programs are supplemented by assistance from universities or other nonprofit organizations. In such cases, outside "helpers" work closely with the school staff, visiting as often as once a week to keep them focused and moving.

We believe that these whole-school efforts make more of a difference than actions focused on only one area or department of a school. However, it is vitally important that the counseling and guidance function be explicitly included. There must not only be a new vision for the school, but a new vision for counseling within the school.

This new vision of school counseling cannot be implemented in a piecemeal or incremental manner. It requires a major shift in the ways in which counselors relate to students, teachers, other staff and administrators, and community members. Such changes will inevitably have ripple effects on other aspects of the school. In this way, modifying counseling is simply a starting place for modifying the education system overall. We have several suggestions for school counselors to help them achieve these goals.

Become Proactive in Meeting Students' Needs

When counselors have a philosophy that expects all students to achieve at the highest levels, their relationships with students will change. Rather than waiting for students to approach them for assistance, counselors will assume a proactive role. They should implement outreach programs designed to inform students about educational opportunities, motivate students to achieve in school, correct any myths and misconceptions that may be holding students back, and provide a range of opportunities for students to develop their talents. Counselors should continually assess students' needs to identify barriers to achievement and should also evaluate the effectiveness of programmatic efforts to remove such barriers.

To reach as many students as possible, counselors should develop networks of service providers, both inside and outside of the school. Participants in these networks will reinforce the basic counseling messages and will enable more students to receive guidance and counseling services. Counselors should therefore exercise their referral skills after identifying, assessing, and (if needed) training a variety of caregivers.

Become Advocates for Students

With Teachers. When counselors act as student advocates in their relationships with teachers, they should consistently affirm each student's potential for achievement and convey the expectation that all members of the school faculty and staff are responsible for helping students develop this potential to the fullest extent. Consistent with this philosophy, counselors should point out where and how teachers are creating obstacles or barriers to student achievement, and help teachers acquire new skills. In addition, counselors should try to work collaboratively with teachers to develop new strategies for increasing students' achievement.

Teachers rarely have the opportunity to observe their colleagues at work. Counselors are among the few staff members with the opportunity to observe and compare diverse teaching styles. The counselor can contribute to improvements in education by sharing with teachers information about what others in the school are doing, so that innovative and effective methods can spread beyond one classroom to the rest of the school.

Counselors should enlist the support and participation of teachers in counseling and guidance. The classroom can be the setting for conveying information (e.g., about graduation or precollege requirements) and for motivating or encouraging students to enroll in rigorous academic programs. This information and support can and should be provided to all students starting as early as junior high school; it should not be restricted only to students in honors, gifted, or precollege courses. If teachers cooperate in this way, more students will have access to guidance resources, the counselor will be able to spend less time conveying routine or standard information, and the teachers will be more likely to accept and internalize the counseling mission.

Counselors see their students only intermittently, but teachers see students on a daily basis. Over the course of a semester or school year, teachers can provide a substantial amount of informal counseling, and students will ask their teachers for guidance. Counselors can help to transform this informal, ad hoc system into an organized, coordinated effort to meet students' needs by training teachers to develop counseling skills. Together, counselors and teachers can identify students' guidance needs and develop approaches for meeting those needs.

With Administrators. Counselors usually react or respond to administrative directives, but they also have a responsibility to educate administrators about goals, philosophies, and skills. Counselors should meet with their principals or assistant principals to point out factors in the school environment that hinder student achievement and to propose cost-effective solutions. They should maintain a focus on achievement by collecting and disseminating information about student outcomes to decision makers. For example, counselors can share information about college-going rates, dropout rates, and percentages of students enrolled in college-preparatory versus remedial classes—all broken down by ethnicity and gender. The implications of such data for education policy and practice can be explored. By collecting and disseminating information about student achievement, counselors can raise questions of equity and access while maintaining a focus on school improvement.

Counselors may need to be more assertive in their dealings with administrators by pointing out that they can be more effective if they are relieved of their quasi-administrative duties. (Of course, they then have the obligation to prove that this is true.) They should also request the opportunity to sit on curriculum and staff-development committees, so they can share with decision makers their philosophies, their observations and analyses of the school, and their ideas for improving student achievement.

With Parents and Community Members.   Rather than assuming that parents who do not contact the school are uninterested in their children's education, counselors should establish outreach programs, initiate contact with parents, and offer support and advice about how parents can help their children succeed in school. Counselors should consider when school programs and conferences are held, and whether the schedules are for the convenience of school personnel or of parents and community members. They should strive to involve parents in planning and decision making, and they should try to offer programs in the language(s) of the parents. Research on parental involvement in education consistently indicates strong positive effects for both students and parents.

In addition, counselors should attempt to enlist the support and participation of a wide range of community organizations, including service agencies, business and civic organizations, clergy, colleges and universities, and individual volunteers (see Herr 1991). As counselors identify and make contact with community organizations and individuals, they can discuss the importance of validating each student's potential and capacity for achievement. Through their interactions with parents and service providers, counselors should strive to promote community involvement in the education process and strengthen community support for student achievement. This will have the dual advantages of increasing the availability and quality of services for students, while encouraging a community culture that emphasizes and values academic achievement.

8

Conclusion

There is optimism about the future of our schools and our children. A particularly encouraging trend is the readiness—even the eagerness—of large numbers of schools to begin systemic change. Increasing numbers of schools recognize the need to reorganize to promote student achievement. They recognize that inadequate education outcomes reflect a troubled system, not inadequate students.

In addition, despite great variation in school reform models and approaches, several elements repeatedly emerge as especially effective in improving student achievement. These include a philosophy that affirms students' capacities for achievement and that establishes high standards for achievement; mobilization of school and community resources to respond to students' intellectual, affective, and behavioral needs; and the development of partnerships among schools, communities, and postsecondary institutions.

Despite these hopeful signs, inequity remains the norm rather than the exception in public education. A member of the Commission on Precollege Guidance and Counseling observed:

> We should state clearly and unequivocally that this country's school system faces the danger of becoming two systems rather than one. One system leads to opportunity through advanced education and interesting careers; the other is for second-level citizens, and it imposes limits, operates on reduced expectations, and manages to discourage and fail more children than it serves well. Counselors alone cannot stop this from happening, but they can become one of the powerful forces arrayed against it. (1986a, p. 29)

The important role of guidance and counseling in middle and secondary schools too often remains unrecognized. Students and their families need:

- encouragement and support;
- advocates who will help them overcome obstacles to high achievement and success in school;
- information about future education and career options; and
- guidance in selecting an academic program that will preserve these options.

The extent to which students have these needs met will largely determine whether they remain in school, achieve at high levels, and enter adulthood prepared to contribute to their families, communities, and country.

Counselors have historically functioned as the gatekeepers of the education system. They have perpetuated educational inequity by assigning poor and minority students to curricula that limit their learning and their options. Instead, counseling and guidance can contribute a great deal to school reform and change. Special efforts are needed to encourage and train counselors to become advocates for students and agents of change for their schools; serve as the education system's "academic conscience"; and maintain a focus on achievement, equity, and opportunity for all students.

Can we change counseling and placement systems? Yes we can. It won't be easy, because these practices are long entrenched, and the profession is highly resistant to change. But there is a warm wind blowing across the educational system. A wind that is sweeping in some very new thinking about what is possible. And is blowing away some of the cobwebs that have clouded the thinking of practicing educators for decades. We worry, however, that those winds won't blow down the high walls that have been built around the counseling and guidance function. That is the danger. But that, too, is the opportunity.

References

American School Counselor Association. (ASCA). 1988. *Position Statement: The School Counselor and Counselor/Student Ratio.* Alexandria, Va.: ASCA.

American School Counselor Association, and National Association of College Admissions Counselors. 1986. *Professional Development Guidelines for Secondary School Counselors: A Self Audit.* Alexandria, Va.: ASCA.

Bastian, A., N. Fruchter, M. Gittell, C. Greer, and K. Haskins. *Choosing Equality: The Case for Democratic Schooling.* Philadelphia: Temple University Press, 1986.

Bobele, M., and T.J. Conran. 1988. "Referrals for Family Therapy: Pitfalls and Guidelines." *Elementary School Guidance and Counseling* February: 192–198.

Boyer, E.L. 1988. "Exploring the Future: Seeking New Challenges." *Journal of College Admissions* 118:2–8.

Burtnett, F. 1988. "School Guidance Programs Should Return to Basics." *School Board News* June 8.

Burtnett, F. 1989. "Counseling and Counselors: A Quest for Quality." *NACAC Bulletin* August: 3, 6–7.

California Postsecondary Education Commission. 1982. *College Participation among Graduates of the Core College Curriculum at Phineas Banning High School,* Sacramento, Calif.: Commission Report 82–28.

California State Department of Education. 1983. *College Core Curriculum: University and College Opportunities Program.* Sacramento, Cal.: California State Department of Education.

California State Department of Education, Office of Special Programs, University and College Opportunities Unit. 1990. *Enhancing Opportunities for Higher Education Among Underrepresented Students: Strategies for High Schools.* Sacramento, Calif.: California State Department of Education.

The Center for Human Resources. 1990. *Future Options Education.* Waltham, Mass.: Brandeis University.

College Entrance Examination Board and the National Association of College Admissions Counselors (NACAC). 1989. *Strengthening Educational Guidance and Counseling in Schools.* A proposal to the Lilly Endowment.

Comer, J. 1986. "Introduction" to Bastian, A., *Choosing Equality.* Philadelphia: Temple University Press.

Commission on Precollege Guidance and Counseling. 1986a. *Keeping the Options Open: An Overview.* New York: College Entrance Examination Board.

Commission on Precollege Guidance and Counseling. 1986b. *Keeping the Options Open: Final Report.* New York: College Entrance Examination Board.

Council for Accreditation of Counseling and Related Educational Programs. 1988. *Accreditation Procedures Manual and Application.* Alexandria, Va.: CACREP.

Epstein, J.L., and K.C. Salinas. 1990. *Promising Programs in Major Academic Subjects in the Middle Grades.* Baltimore: Center for Research on Effective Schooling for Disadvantaged Students, The Johns Hopkins University.

Finn, C.E., Jr. 1991. *We Must Take Charge: Our Schools and Our Future.* New York: The Free Press.

Ekstrom, R.B. 1985. A Descriptive Study of Public High School Guidance: Final report to the Commission for the Study of Precollegiate Guidance and Counseling. Princeton, N.J.: Educational Testing Service (unpublished paper).

George, C.A. 1989. *A Summary Report of Course Enrollment Practices of High School Students in Southern California.* Sacramento: California State Department of Education.

Gysbers, N.C., and P. Henderson. 1988. *Developing and Managing Your School Guidance Program.* Alexandria, Va.: American Association for Counseling and Development.

Hannaford, M.J. 1987. "Balancing the Counseling Program to Meet School Needs." *NASSP Bulletin* May: 3–9.

Hart, P.J. 1990. *Leadership Seminar* (an address to staff in the California State Department of Education—Compensatory Education). Sacramento, Calif.: September 19.

Hart, P.J., and J. Mayes. 1984. *A Thought Piece on Counseling* (unpublished paper prepared for the Planning Committee of The Achievement Council). Los Angeles.

Hartman, K.E. 1988. "Clarifying the Role of School Counselors." *Education Week* June 1: 32.

Hartman, R.A.H. 1988. "A Counselor Role: Curriculum Development and Evaluation." *The School Counselor* 35 May: 377–382.

Haycock, K., and M.S. Navarro. 1988. *Unfinished Business: Fulfilling Our Children's Promise.* Los Angeles: The Achievement Council.

Herr, E. 1986. *School Counselor Training in Precollege Guidance and Counseling* (unpublished paper prepared for the Commission on Precollege Guidance and Counseling).

Herr, E. 1991. *Guidance and Counseling: A Shared Responsibility.* Alexandria, Va.: National Association of College Admissions Counselors (NACAC).

Higher Education Information Center. *Make It Happen!* Boston: The Education Resources Institute.

Higher Education Information Center. 1991. *Meeting the Challenges of the 1990s: 1990 in Review.* Boston: Higher Education Information Center.

Lee, V.E., and R.B. Ekstrom. 1987. "Student Access to Guidance Counseling in High School." *American Educational Research Journal* 24: 287–310.

Mayer, D. 1991. *Do Early Educational Awareness Programs Increase the Chances of Eighth Graders Reaching Higher Education?* Boston: Higher Education Information Center of the Education Resources Institute (unpublished paper).

Moles, O.C. 1991. "Guidance Programs in American High Schools: A Descriptive Portrait." *The School Counselor* 38: 163–177.

Monson, R.J., and D. Brown. 1985. "Secondary School Counseling: A Time for Reassessment and Revitalization." *NASSP Bulletin* December: 32–35.

A Nation at Risk: The Imperative for Educational Reform. 1983. Washington, D.C.: U.S. Government Printing Office.

National Association of College Admissions Counselors. 1991. *Statement on Counselor Competencies.* Alexandria, Va.: NACAC.

National Association of Student Financial Aid Administrators (NASFAA) and American Council on Education (ACE). 1989. *Certainty of Opportunity: A Report on the NASFAA/ACE Symposium on Early Awareness of Postsecondary Education.* Washington, D.C.: NASFAA.

National Board of Certified Counselors. 1991. NBCC Counselor Certification: National Certified School Counselor Information and Application. Alexandria, Va.: NBCC.

National Board for Professional Teaching Standards. 1990. *Toward High and Rigorous Standards for the Teaching Profession: Initial Policies and Perspectives of the National Board for Professional Teaching Standards,* 2nd ed. Washington, D.C.: National Board for Professional Teaching Standards.

National Board for Professional Teaching Standards. 1991. *1990 Annual Report.* Washington, D.C.: National Board for Professional Teaching Standards.

National Center for Education Statistics. 1990. *Digest of Education Statistics 1990.* Washington, D.C.: U.S. Department of Education.

National College Counseling Project. 1986. *Frontiers of Possibility.* Alexandria, Va.: National Association of College Admissions Counselors (NACAC).

Oakes, J. 1985. *Keeping Track: How Schools Structure Inequity.* New Haven: Yale University Press.

Olson, L. 1991. "Shortcomings in School Based Management in Boston Noted." *Education Week.* XI September 25: 5.

O'Neil, J. 1991. "Transforming the Curriculum for Students 'At Risk.' " *Curriculum Update* June 1991: 1–3, 6–8.

Palo Alto Pupil Personnel Services. 1990. Study Session. Comprehensive Health and Human Services: Our Challenge and Opportunity. Presentation Board of Education, Palo Alto Unified School District (March).

Partners for Educational Excellence. 1990. *Program Guidelines.* Winter Park, Fla.: Rollins College.

Rosenbaum, J.E. 1976. *Making Inequality: The Hidden Current of High School Tracking.* New York: Wiley.

Schmidt, P. 1991. "New Jersey to Implement Comer Program in Urban Districts." *Education Week* XI September 18: 20.

Sizer, T.R., and H.M. Houston. 1985. *The Coalition of Essential Schools: Prospects.* Providence, R.I.: Brown University.

Stigler, J.W., and H.W. Stevenson. 1991. "How Asian Teachers Polish Each Lesson to Perfection." *American Educator* 15: 12–20.

Texas Education Agency. 1990. *The Comprehensive Guidance Program for Texas Public Schools: A Guide for Program Development Pre-K–12th Grades.* Austin, Tex.: Texas Education Agency.

Appendix A

Selected Data on Counselors and Counselor Training

Guidance Counselors by Gender

Public/Private/Catholic Schools	Males	Females	Unknown	Total
Elementary Schools	8,441	25,153	2,149	35,743
Middle/Junior High Schools	6,358	10,432	795	17,585
Senior High, Voc-Tech Schools	16,963	19,556	1,450	37,969
Combined (K–12) Schools	2,252	2,806	229	5,287
Adult Schools	275	330	20	625
Special Education Schools	603	1,036	227	1,866
Total	34,892	59,313	4,870	99,075

Source: Market Data Retrieval, Shelton, Connecticut.

Counselor Education at the Master's Degree Level (1990)

Title of Major	Number of Majors Identified	Number of Programs Reporting Information for Males	Male Graduates	Number of Programs Reporting Information for Females	Female Graduates	Average Number of Graduates per Program		
						Males	Females	Total
Counseling Psychology	35	28	276	28	507	9.9	18.1	28.0
Marital and Family Therapy								
Marital and Family Counseling	30	21	107	21	207	5.1	9.9	15.0
Mental Health Counseling	160	130	965	128	1,939	7.4	15.2	22.6
Agency Counseling								
Community Counseling								
Counseling								
Counseling the Elderly								
Human Development Counseling								
Rehabilitation Counseling	61	57	292	58	607	5.1	10.5	15.6
School Counseling	263	211	1,310	211	3,114	6.2	15.0	21.2
Elementary School Counseling								
Guidance Counseling								
Secondary School Counseling								
Substance Abuse Counseling	11	5	34	6	43	5.7	7.2	12.9
Drug and Alcohol Abuse Counseling								
Average						6.6	14.2	20.8
Total	560	452	2,984	452	6,417			

Source: *Counselor Preparation 1990–92: Programs, Personnel, Trends* (7th ed.) (Muncie, In: Accelerated Development, Inc., 1991).

Appendix B

Programs with CACREP Accreditation in School Counseling

Alabama
Counseling and Counseling Psychology
2014 Haley Center
Auburn University
Auburn University, AL 36849-5222

Counselor Education
Graves Hall
University of Alabama
P.O. Box 870231
Tuscaloosa, AL 35487-0231

British Columbia
Department of Counseling Psychology
University of British Columbia
5780 Toronto Road
Vancouver, B.C. Canada V6T 1L2

California
Division of Administration and
   Counseling
California State University/Los Angeles
5151 State University Drive
Los Angeles, CA 90032

Educational Psychology and Counseling
California State University/Northridge
1811 Nordhoff Street
Northridge, CA 91330

Department of Counseling
California State University/Sacramento
6000 J Street
Sacramento, CA 95819

Department of Counseling
San Francisco State University
1600 Holloway Avenue
San Francisco, CA 94132

Counseling Department
Nichols 220
Sonoma State University
1801 East Cotati Avenue
Rohnert Park, CA 94928

Colorado
Division of Counseling and Personnel
  Services
School of Education
P.O. Box 173364
Campus Box 106
University of Colorado at Denver
Denver, CO 80217-3364

Counseling Psychology Program
Division of Professional Psychology
McKee Hall #248
University of Northern Colorado
Greeley, CO 80639

Connecticut
Community and School Counseling
Graduate School of Education and
  Allied Professions
Fairfield University
Fairfield, CT 06430-7524

District of Columbia
Department of Human Services
T605 Academic Center
George Washington University
801 22nd Street, N.W.
Washington, D.C. 20052

Florida
Department of Counselor Education
1215 Norman Hall
University of Florida
Gainesville, FL 32611

Georgia
Counseling and Psychological Services
University Plaza
Georgia State University
Atlanta, GA 30303-3083

Counseling and Human Development
  Services
402 Aderhold Hall
University of Georgia
Athens, GA 30602

Hawaii
Department of Counselor Education
Room 222, Wist Hall Annex 2
University of Hawaii at Manoa
1776 University Avenue
Honolulu, HI 96822

Idaho
Department of Counselor Education and
  Special Education
Idaho State University
Box 8059
Pocatello, ID 83209

Counseling and Special Education
University of Idaho
Moscow, ID 83843

Illinois
Bradley University
Department of Educational Leadership
  and Human Development
Westlake Hall
Peoria, IL 61625

Division of Psychology and Counseling
College of Education
Governors State University
University Park, IL 60466

Department of Specialized Educational
  Development
College of Education
Fairchild Hall
Illinois State University
Normal, IL 61761-6901

Educational Psychology, Counseling,
  and Special Education
Northern Illinois University
Graham Hall 223
DeKalb, IL 60115-2854

Counseling Programs
Department of Educational Psychology
Southern Illinois University
Carbondale, IL 62901-4618

Department of Counselor Education and
  College Student Personnel
Western Illinois University
74 Horrabin Hall
Macomb, IL 61455

Indiana
Counseling and Development
Engineering Administration Building
Purdue University
West Lafayette, IN 47907

Iowa
Educational Administration and
    Counseling
University of Northern Iowa
508 Education Center
Cedar Falls, IA 50614-0604

Division of Counselor Education
N338 Lindquist Center
University of Iowa
Iowa City, IA 52242

Louisiana
College of Education
Northeast Louisiana University
700 University Avenue
Monroe, LA 71209-0205

Educational Leadership and
    Foundations
University of New Orleans
Lakefront
New Orleans, LA 70148

Maine
Department of Human Resource
    Development
400 Bailey Hall
University of Southern Maine
Gorham, ME 04038

Michigan
Educational and Counseling Psychology
Bell Hall 160
Andrews University
Berrien Springs, MI 49104-1000

Counselor Education and Counseling
    Psychology
3102 Sangren Hall
Western Michigan University
Kalamazoo, MI 49008-5195

Minnesota
Counseling and Student Personnel
MSU Box 52
Mankato State University
P.O. Box 8400
Mankato, MN 56002-8400

Mississippi
Department of Counselor Education
P.O. Drawer GE
Mississippi State University
Mississippi State, MS 39762

Missouri
Counselor Preparation, 8H #104
Northeast Missouri State University
Kirksville, MO 63501

Nevada
Counseling and Educational Psychology
University of Nevada/Las Vegas
4505 Maryland Parkway
Las Vegas, NV 89154-3003

New Jersey
Counseling and Personnel Services
Trenton State College
Trenton, NJ 08650-4700

New Mexico
Counseling and Family Studies
College of Education
University of New Mexico
Albuquerque, NM 87131

New York
Counseling and Development
Long Island University/C.W. Post
    Campus
Brookville, NY 11548

Center for Human Resources
State University of New York/
    Plattsburgh
Plattsburgh, NY 12901

Department of Counselor Education
Faculty Office Building
State University of New York College at
    Brockport
Brockport, NY 14420

North Carolina
Human Development and Psychology
    Counseling
Appalachian State University
Boone, NC 28608

Counseling and Psychology
CB #3500, 107 Peabody Hall
University of North Carolina/Chapel Hill
Chapel Hill, NC 25799-3500

Department of Counseling and
    Specialized Educational Development
228 Curry Building
University of North Carolina/Greensboro
Greensboro, NC 27412-5001

Ohio
Department of Counselor Education
313C McCracken Hall
Ohio University
Athens, OH 45701

Counseling and Special Education
127 Carroll Hall
University of Akron
Akron, OH 44325-5007

Department of Counselor and Human
   Education
University of Toledo
2801 West Bancroft Street
Toledo, OH 43606

Department of Human Services
Wright State University
Dayton, OH 45435

Department of Counseling
Youngstown State University
410 Wick Avenue
Youngstown, OH 44555

Oregon
Department of Counseling
Education Hall 315
Oregon State University/Western
   Oregon State University
Corvallis, OR 97331

Pennsylvania
Department of Counseling
Shippensburg University
North Prince Street
Shippensburg, PA 17257

Psychology in Education
5C-01 Forbes Quadrangle
University of Pittsburgh
Pittsburgh, PA 15260

Department of Human Resources
University of Scranton
Scranton, PA 18510

Education and Human Services
Suite 302-308 Falvey Hall
Villanova University
Villanova, PA 19085

South Carolina
Department of Educational Psychology
Education Building
University of South Carolina/Columbia
Columbia, SC 29208

Tennessee
Educational and Counseling Psychology
108 Claxton Education Building
University of Tennessee/Knoxville
Knoxville, TN 37996-3400

Department of Human Resources
Box 322, Peabody College
Vanderbilt University
Nashville, TN 37203

Texas
Department of Counseling and
   Guidance
East Texas State University
Commerce, TX 75429

Department of Counselor Education
P.O. Box 13857
University of North Texas
Denton, TX 76203-3857

Vermont
Department of Organizational,
   Counseling, and Foundational
   Studies
405 Waterman Building
University of Vermont
Burlington, VT 05405-0160

Virginia
Department of Counselor Education
1501 Lakeside Drive
Lynchburg College
Lynchburg, VA 24501-3199

Counselor Education Program
169 Ruffner Hall
University of Virginia
Charlottesville, VA 22903

Wisconsin
Department of Counselor Education
University of Wisconsin Oshkosh
Oshkosh, WI 54901

Wyoming
Department of Counselor Education
P.O. Box 3374, University Station
University of Wyoming
Laramie, WY 82071